First Workshop on Interactive and Executable Semantic Parsing (IntEx-SemPar 2020)

Online
19 November 2020

ISBN: 978-1-7138-1986-8

Printed from e-media with permission by:

Curran Associates, Inc.
57 Morehouse Lane
Red Hook, NY 12571

Some format issues inherent in the e-media version may also appear in this print version.

Printed with permission by Curran Associates, Inc. (2021)

For permission requests, please contact the Association for Computational Linguistics at the address below.

Association for Computational Linguistics
209 N. Eighth Street
Stroudsburg, Pennsylvania 18360

Phone: 1-570-476-8006
Fax: 1-570-476-0860

acl@aclweb.org

Additional copies of this publication are available from:

Curran Associates, Inc.
57 Morehouse Lane
Red Hook, NY 12571 USA
Phone: 845-758-0400
Fax: 845-758-2633
Email: curran@proceedings.com
Web: www.proceedings.com

EMNLP 2020

Interactive and Executable Semantic Parsing

Proceedings of the First Workshop

November 19, 2020
Online

Introduction

Welcome to the First Workshop on Interactive and Executable Semantic Parsing (IntEx-SemPar 2020)!

Executable semantic parsers map natural language utterances to meaning representations that can be executed in a particular context such as databases, knowledge graphs, robotic environment, and software applications. It has become increasingly important as it allows users to seek information and control computer systems naturally and flexibly via interactive exchanges in natural language. We envision that practical semantic parsing systems need to be equipped with three core capabilities: (1) Understanding user utterances in context and mapping them to executable forms. (2) Clarifying ambiguous utterances and providing guidance for user to form valid input. (3) Providing a faithful explanation of its interpreted actions for user verification and feedback. To this end, the problem of mapping well-formed, individual natural language utterances to formal representations has been studied extensively. In comparison, semantic parsing in an interactive setup has received less attention until very recently. Furthermore, most of existing semantic parsers assume valid input only hence cannot detect ambiguous/invalid utterances and clarify them effectively. There is also less focus on explainability and trustworthiness, where the system can explain its interpreted actions to the user for verification and feedback.

The goal of this workshop is to bring together researchers and promote exciting work towards powerful, robust, and reliable interactive executable semantic parsing systems. Through a rigorous review process, out of 14 submissions, we accept 9 papers (3 non-archival and 6 archival). These papers explore different aspects of semantic parsing in different application scenarios including robustness in Text-to-SQL systems, explainability and interpretability in Knowledge Graphs, uncertainty and active learning in Task-Oriented Dialog, adaptive language interfaces through decomposition, pretrainig models for table semantic parsing, analysis in open-domain semantic parsing.

Furthermore, this workshop is featured with a strong and diverse lineup of invited speakers from areas spanning semantic parsing, dialogue systems, grounded language learning, robotics, and program synthesis. Yoav Artzi from Cornell has contributed significantly to natural language learning in situated interactions. Jonathan Berant from Tel-Aviv University has made pioneer work in semantic parsing and question answering under weak supervision. Richard Socher is a world-renowned researcher in Natural Language Processing, computer vision, Deep Learning, and Artificial Intelligence. Dilek Hakkani-Tür has made fundamental contributions to spoken dialog and conversation modeling and she is currently leading the Amazon Alexa AI team. Alex Polozov from Microsoft Research is a leading researcher in neural program synthesis from input-output examples and natural language. Jacob Andreas is a leading researcher from MIT working on building intelligent systems that can communicate effectively using language and learn from human guidance.

We hope you enjoy this rich program and contribute to the future success of this field!

IntEx-SemPar 2020 Organizers
Ben Bogin, Tel Aviv University
Srinivasan Iyer, University of Washington
Victoria Lin, Salesforce Research
Dragomir Radev, Yale University
Alane Suhr, Cornell University
Panupong (Ice) Pasupat, Google
Caiming Xiong, Salesforce Research
Pengcheng Yin, Carnegie Mellon University
Tao Yu, Yale University
Rui Zhang, Penn State University
Victor Zhong, University of Washington

Steering Committee:

Jonathan Berant, Tel-Aviv University
Graham Neubig, Carnegie Mellon University
Yunyao Li, IBM Research
Caiming Xiong, Salesforce Research
Dragomir Radev, Yale University
Luke Zettlemoyer, University of Washington

Organizing Committee:

Ben Bogin, Tel Aviv University
Srinivasan Iyer, University of Washington
Victoria Lin, Salesforce Research
Alane Suhr, Cornell University
Panupong (Ice) Pasupat, Google
Pengcheng Yin, Carnegie Mellon University
Tao Yu, Yale University
Rui Zhang, Penn State University
Victor Zhong, University of Washington

Program Committee:

Siva Reddy, MILA/McGill University
Michihiro Yasunaga, Stanford
Bailin Wang, University of Edinburgh
Luheng He, Google Research
Ziyu Yao, OSU
Izzeddin Gur, Google Research
Eran Yahav, Technion
Chien-Sheng Wu, Salesforce Research
Uri Alon, Technion
Giovanni Campagna, Stanford University
Chenglong Wang, University of Washington
Catherine Finegan-Dollak, IBM Research
Semih Yavuz, Salesforce Research
Matt Gardner, AI2
Raymond Mooney, UT-Austin
Richard Shin, UC-Berkeley
He He, New York University
Yansong Feng, Peking University
Li Dong, Microsoft Research
Chen Liang, Google Brain
Yibo Sun, Harbin Institute of Technology
Zhou Yu, UC-Davis
Jonathan Herzig, Tel Aviv University
Wei Lu, SUTD
Mirella Lapata, University of Edinburgh
Jonathan Kummerfeld, UMich-Ann Arbor
Zhanming Jie, SUTD

Miltiadis Allamanis, Microsoft Research
Eunsol Choi, Google/UT-Austin
Yu Su, Microsoft Semantic Machines/OSU
Scott Yih, Facebook AI Research
Silei Xu, Stanford
Yi Chern Tan, Yale
Shuaichen Chang, OSU
Tianze Shi, Cornell
Songhe Wang, UNC
Ansong Ni, Yale
Chang Shu, University of Edinburgh
Ruiqi Zhong, UC-Berkeley
Peng Shi, University of Waterloo
Yusen Zhang, Emory University

Table of Contents

QA2Explanation: Generating and Evaluating Explanations for Question Answering Systems over Knowledge Graph
Saeedeh Shekarpour, Abhishek Nadgeri and Kuldeep Singh 1

Uncertainty and Traffic-Aware Active Learning for Semantic Parsing
Priyanka Sen and Emine Yilmaz 12

Improving Sequence-to-Sequence Semantic Parser for Task Oriented Dialog
Chaoting Xuan 18

Learning Adaptive Language Interfaces through Decomposition
Siddharth Karamcheti, Dorsa Sadigh and Percy Liang 23

ColloQL: Robust Text-to-SQL Over Search Queries
Karthik Radhakrishnan, Arvind Srikantan and Xi Victoria Lin 34

Natural Language Response Generation from SQL with Generalization and Back-translation
Saptarashmi Bandyopadhyay and Tianyang Zhao 46

Conference Program

For final program, check https://intex-sempar.github.io/

Thursday, November 19, 2020

08:15–08:30 Opening remarks

08:30–09:30 Invited Talk: Jacob Andreas

09:30–10:30 Invited Talk: Jonathan Berant

10:30–10:50 Break

10:50–11:00 *Learning Adaptive Language Interfaces through Decomposition*
Siddharth Karamcheti, Dorsa Sadigh, and Percy Liang

11:00–11:10 *Improving Sequence-to-Sequence Semantic Parser for Task Oriented Dialog*
Chaoting Xuan

11:10–11:20 *Uncertainty and Traffic-Aware Active Learning for Semantic Parsing*
Priyanka Sen and Emine Yilmaz

11:20–11:30 *Did You Ask a Good Question? A Cross-Domain Question Intention Classification Benchmark for Text-to-SQL*
Yusen Zhang, Xiangyu Dong, Shuaichen Chang, Tao Yu, Peng Shi, and Rui Zhang

11:30–12:30 Invited Talk: Yoav Artzi

12:30–13:30 Poster Presentation

13:30–14:30 Invited Talk: Dilek Hakkani-Tür

14:30–14:40 *QA2Explanation: Generating and Evaluating Explanations for Question Answering Systems over Knowledge Graph*
Saeedeh Shekarpour, Abhishek Nadgeri, and Kuldeep Singh

14:40–14:50 *ColloQL: Robust Text-to-SQL Over Search Queries*
Karthik Radhakrishnan, Arvind Srikantan, and Xi Victoria Lin

14:50–15:00 *GraPPa: Grammar-Augmented Pre-Training for Table Semantic Parsing*
Tao Yu, Chien-Sheng Wu, Xi Victoria Lin, Bailin Wang, Yi Chern Tan, Xinyi Yang, Dragomir Radev, Richard Socher, and Caiming Xiong

(Continue)

Thursday, November 19, 2020

15:00–15:10	*Re-thinking Open-domain Semantic Parsing* Yu Gu, Sue Kase, Michelle Vanni, Brian Sadler, Percy Liang, Xifeng Yan, and Yu Su
15:10–15:20	*Natural Language Response Generation from SQL with Generalization and Back-translation* Saptarashmi Bandyopadhyay and Tianyang Zhao
15:20–15:30	Break
15:30–16:30	Invited Talk: Alex Polozov
16:30–17:30	Invited Talk: Richard Socher
17:30–17:35	Closing remarks

QA2Explanation: Generating and Evaluating Explanations for Question Answering Systems over Knowledge Graph

Saeedeh Shekarpour
University of Dayton
Dayton, USA
sshekarpour1
@udayton.edu

Abhishek Nadgeri
RWTH Aachen &
Zerotha Research, Germany
abhishek.nadgeri
@rwth-aachen.de

Kuldeep Singh
Cerence GmbH &
Zerotha Research, Germany
kuldeep.singh1
@cerence.com

Abstract

In the era of Big Knowledge Graphs, Question Answering (QA) systems have reached a milestone in their performance and feasibility. However, their applicability, particularly in specific domains such as the biomedical domain, has not gained wide acceptance due to their "black box" nature, which hinders transparency, fairness, and accountability of QA systems. Therefore, users are unable to understand how and why particular questions have been answered, whereas some others fail. To address this challenge, in this paper, we develop an automatic approach for generating explanations during various stages of a pipeline-based QA system. Our approach is a supervised and automatic approach which considers three classes (i.e., success, no answer, and wrong answer) for annotating the output of involved QA components. Upon our prediction, a template explanation is chosen and integrated into the output of the corresponding component. To measure the effectiveness of the approach, we conducted a user survey as to how non-expert users perceive our generated explanations. The results of our study show a significant increase in the four dimensions of the human factor from the Human-computer interaction community.

1 Introduction

The recent advances of Question Answering (QA) technologies mostly rely on (i) the advantages of Big Knowledge Graphs which augment the semantics, structure, and accessibility of data, *e.g.,* Web of Data has published around 150B triples from a variety of domains[1], and (ii) the competency of contemporary AI approaches which train sophisticated learning models (statistical models (Shekarpour et al., 2015, 2013), neural networks (Lukovnikov et al., 2017), and attention models (Liu, 2019)) on a large size of training data, and given a variety of novel features captured from semantics, structure, and context of the background data. However, similar to other branches of AI applications, the state of the art of QA systems are *"black boxes"* that fail to provide transparent explanations about why a particular answer is generated. This black box behavior diminishes the confidence and trust of the user and hinders the reliance and acceptance of the black-box systems, especially in critical domains such as healthcare, biomedical, life-science, and self-driving cars (Samek et al., 2017; Miller, 2018). The running hypothesis in this paper is that the lack of explanation for answers provided by QA systems diminishes the trust and acceptance of the user towards these systems. Therefore, by implementing more transparent, interpretable, or explainable QA systems, the end users will be better equipped to justify and therefore trust the output of QA systems (Li et al., 2018).

Furthermore, **data quality** is a critical factor that highly affects the performance of QA systems. In other words, when the background data is flawed or outdated, it undermines the humanlikeness and acceptance of the QA systems if no explanation is provided, especially for non-expert users. For example, the SINA engine (Shekarpour et al., 2015) failed to answer the simple question *"What is the population of Canada?"* on the DBpedia (Auer et al., 2007) version 2013, whereas it succeeded for similar questions such as *"What is the population of Germany?"*. The error analysis showed that the expected triple *i.e.,* `<dbr[2]:Canada dbo[3]:population "xxx">` is missing from DBpedia 2013. Thus, if the QA system does not provide any explanation about such failures, then the non-expert user concludes the QA system into the demerit points. Thus, in general, the errors or

[1] `http://lodstats.aksw.org/`

[2] dbr is bound to `http://dbpedia.org/resource/`.

[3] The prefix dbo is bound to `http://dbpedia.org/ontology/`.

Proceedings of the First Workshop on Interactive and Executable Semantic Parsing, pages 1–11
Online, November 19, 2020. ©2020 Association for Computational Linguistics
https://doi.org/10.18653/v1/P17

failures of the QA systems might be caused by the inadequacies of the underlying data or misunderstanding, misinterpretation, or miscomputation of the employed computational models. In either case, the black-box QA system does not provide any explanations regarding the sources of the error. Often the research community obsesses with the technical discussion of QA systems and competes on enhancing the performance of the QA systems, whereas, on the downside of the QA systems, there is a human who plays a vital role in the acceptance of the system. The Human-Computer Interaction (HCI) community already targeted various aspects of the human-centered design and evaluation challenges of black-box systems. However, the QA systems over KGs received the least attention comparing to other AI applications such as recommender systems (Herlocker et al., 2000; Kouki et al., 2017).

Motivation and Approach: Plethora of QA systems over knowledge graphs developed in the last decade (Höffner et al., 2017). These QA systems are evaluated on various benchmarking datasets including WebQuestions (Berant et al., 2013), QALD (Unger et al., 2015), LC-QuAD (Trivedi et al., 2017), and report results based on global metrics of precision, recall, and F-score. In many cases, QA approaches over KGs even surpass the human level performance (Petrochuk and Zettlemoyer, 2018). Irrespective of the underlying technology and algorithms, these QA systems act as black box and do not provide any explanation to the user regarding 1) why a particular answer is generated and 2) how the given answer is extracted from the knowledge source. The recent works towards explainable artificial intelligence (XAI) gained momentum because several AI applications find limited acceptance due to ethical reasons (Angwin et al., 2016) and a lack of trust on behalf of their users (Stubbs et al., 2007). The same rationale is also applicable to the black-box QA systems. Research studies showed that representing adequate explanations to the answer brings acceptability and confidence to the user as observed in various domains such as recommender systems and visual question answering (Herlocker et al., 2000; Hayes and Shah, 2017; Hendricks et al., 2016; Wu and Mooney, 2018). In this paper, we argue that having explanations increases the trustworthiness, transparency, and acceptance of the answers of the QA system over KGs. Especially, when the QA systems fail to answer a question or provide a wrong answer, the explanatory output helps to keep the user informed about a particular behavior. Hence, we propose a template-based explanation generation approach for QA systems. Our proposed approach for explainable QA system over KG provides (i) *adequate justification:* thus the end user feels that they are aware of the reasoning steps of the computational model, (ii) *confidence:* the user can trust the system and has the willing for the continuation of interactions, (iii) *understandability:* educates the user as how the system infers or what are the causes of failures and unexpected answers, and (iv) *user involvement:* encourages the user to engage in the process of QA such as question rewriting.

Research Questions: We deal with two key research questions about the explanations of the QA systems as follows: **RQ1:** *What is an effective model and scheme for automatically generating explanations?* The computational model employed in a QA system might be extremely complicated. The exposure of the depth of details will not be sufficient for the end user. The preference is to generate natural language explanations that are readable and understandable to the non-expert user. **RQ2:** *How is the perception of end users about explanations along the human factor dimensions?*, which is whether or not the explanations establish confidence, justification, understanding, and further engagements of the user.

Our key contributions are: 1) a scheme for shallow explanatory QA pipeline systems, 2) a method for automatically generating explanations, and 3) a user survey to measure the human factors of user perception from explanations. This paper is organized as follows: In Section 2, we review the related work. Section 3 explains the major concepts of the QA pipeline system, which is our employed platform. Section 4 provides our presentation and detailed discussion of the proposed approach. Our experimental study is presented in Section 5, followed by a discussion Section. We conclude the paper in section 7.

2 Related Work

Researchers have tackled the problem of question answering in various domains including open domain question answering (Yang et al., 2019), biomedical (Bhandwaldar and Zadrozny, 2018), geospatial (Punjani et al., 2018), and temporal (Jia et al., 2018). Question answering over publicly available KGs is a long-standing field with over 62 QA systems developed since 2010 (Höffner et al., 2017). The implementation of various QA systems can be broadly categorized into three approaches (Singh, 2019; Diefenbach et al., 2018). The first is a semantic parsing based approach such as (Usbeck et al., 2015) that implements a QA system using several linguistic analyses (e.g., POS tagging, dependency parsing) and linked data technologies. The second approach is an end-to-end machine learning based, which uses a large amount of training data to map an input question to its answer directly (e.g., in (Yang et al., 2019; Lukovnikov et al., 2017)). The third approach is based on modular frameworks (Kim et al., 2017; Singh et al., 2018b) which aims at reusing individual modules of QA systems, independent tools (such as entity linking, predicate linking) in building QA systems collaboratively. Irrespective of the implementation approach, domain, and the underlying knowledge source (KG, documents, relational tables, etc.), the majority of existing QA systems act as a black box. The reason behind black box behavior is due to either the monolithic tightly coupled modules such as in semantic parsing based QA systems or nested and nonlinear structure of machine learning based algorithms employed in QA systems. The modular framework, on the other hand, provides flexibility to track individual stages of the answer generation process. The rationale behind our choice of the modular framework over monolithic QA systems is a flexible architecture design of such frameworks. It allows us to trace failure at each stage of the QA pipeline. We enrich the output of each step with adequate justification with supporting natural language explanation for the user. Hence, as the first step towards explainable QA over knowledge graphs, we propose an automatic approach for generating a description for each stage of a QA pipeline in a state-of-the-art modular framework (in our case: Frankenstein (Singh et al., 2018b)). We are not aware of any work in the direction of explainable question answering over knowledge graphs and we make the first attempt in this paper. Although, efforts have been made to explain visual question answering systems. Some works generate textual explanations for VQA by training a recurrent neural network (RNN) to mimic examples of human descriptions (Hendricks et al., 2016; Wu and Mooney, 2018) directly. The work by (Ngonga Ngomo et al., 2013) can be considered a closest attempt to our work. The authors proposed a template based approach to translate SPARQL queries into natural language verbalization. We employ a similar template-based approach to generate an automatic explanation for QA pipelines.

In other domains, such as expert systems, the earlier attempts providing explanations to the users can be traced back in the early 70s (Shortliffe, 1974). Since then, extensive work has been done to include explanations in expert systems followed by recommender systems to explain the system's knowledge of the domain and the reasoning processes these systems employ to produce results (for details, please refer to (Moore and Swartout, 1988; Jannach et al., 2010; Daher et al., 2017). For a recommender system, work by (Herlocker et al., 2000) is an early attempt to evaluate different implementations of explanation interfaces in "MovieLens" recommender system. Simple statements provided to the customers as explanations mentioning the similarity to other highly rated films or a favorite actor or actress were among the best recommendations of the MovieLens system compared to the unexplained recommendations. Furthermore, applications of explanation are also considered in various sub-domains of artificial intelligence, such as justifying medical decision-making (Fox et al., 2007), explaining autonomous agent behavior (Hayes and Shah, 2017), debugging of machine learning models (Kulesza et al., 2015), and explaining predictions of classifiers (Ribeiro et al., 2016).

3 QA Pipeline on Knowledge Graph

One of the implementation approaches for answering questions from interlinked knowledge graphs is typically a multi-stage process which is called *QA pipeline* (Singh et al., 2018b). Each stage of the pipeline deals with a required task such as Named Entity Recognition (NER) and Disambiguation (NED) (referred as Entity Linking (EL)), Relation extraction and Linking (RL), and Query Building (QB). There is an abundance of components performing QA tasks (Diefenbach et al., 2018). These implementations run on the KGs and have been developed based on AI, NLP, and Semantic Technologies, which accomplish one or more tasks of a QA pipeline (Höffner et al., 2017). Table 1 (Singh et al., 2018b) presents performance of best QA components on the LC-QuAD dataset, implementing QA tasks. The components are Tag Me API (Ferragina and Scaiella, 2010)) for NED, RL (Relation Linking) implemented by RNLIWOD[4] and SPARQL query builder by NLIWOD QB[5]). For example, given the question *"Did Tesla win a nobel prize in physics?"*, the ideal NED component is expected to recognize the keyword *"Tesla"* as a named entity and map it to the corresponding DBpedia resource, i.e. `dbr:Nikola_Tesla`. Similarly, the multi-word unit *"nobel prize in physics"* has to be linked to `dbr:Nobel_Prize_in_Physics`. Thereafter, a component performing RL finds embedded relations in the given question and links them to appropriate relations of the underlying knowledge graph. In our example, the keyword *"win"* is mapped to the relation `dbo:award`. Finally, the QB component generates a formal query (e.g. expressed in SPARQL) (i.e. `ASK {dbr:Nikola_Tesla dbo:award dbr:Nobel_Prize_in_Physics.}`). The performance values in Table 1 are averaged over the entire query inventory.

Table 1: Performance of QA components implementing various QA tasks on LC-QuAD dataset.

QA Component	QA Task	Precision	Recall	F-Score
TagMe	NED	0.69	0.66	0.67
RNLIWOD	RL	0.25	0.22	0.23
NLIWOD QB	QB	0.48	0.49	0.48

4 Approach

A full QA pipeline is required to answer a given question q. Such QA pipelines are composed of all the required components performing necessary tasks to transform a user-supplied natural language (NL) question into a formal query language (*i.e.,* SPARQL). We consider three generic classes for outputs of a full QA pipeline or individual components, namely $O_c = \{Success, NoAnswer, WrongAnswer\}$. Concerning a given question, a "success" class is when the QA pipeline (component) successfully provides a correct output, a "No Answer" class happens when the full QA pipeline (or an individual component) does not return any output and "Wrong Answer" class is when the provided output is incorrect.

To address **RQ1**, we introduce a scheme for generating explanations for the QA pipeline system. This scheme produces shallow, however automatic explanations using a semi-supervised approach for generating individual explanations after running each integrated component. In our proposed model, the class of the output of each integrated component is predicted using a supervised learning approach. We train a classifier per component within the pipeline. Then based on the prediction of the classifier, an explanation template is chosen. The explanation template and the output of the component are incorporated to form the final representation of explanations. We have a repository of explanation templates for each component of the QA pipeline system. For example, the NED component corresponds to several explanation templates differing based on the number of the output entities. Precisely, the explanation template when the NED has one single entity is different from when it has two or three. Moreover, the templates vary based on the Part of Speach (POS) tag of the entities recognized in the input question. For example, Figure 1 shows a pipeline containing three components: 1) NED component: TagMe, 2) RL component: RNLIWOD QB, and 3) QB component: NLIWOD QB. Three classifiers were individually trained for each component. In this example, for the given question *"Did Tesla win a nobel prize in physics?"* the classifiers predicted the class of "Success" for NED and the class "No Answer" for RL and QB components. Thus, the explanation templates corresponding to the class of "success" for NED, and "No Answer" for RL and QB are filtered. Then since the NED component has two outputs, therefore, two explanations were generated for NED, whereas the remaining components show one explanation.

4.1 Predicting Output of Components

The set of necessary QA tasks formalized as $\mathcal{T} = \{t_1, t_2, \ldots, t_n\}$ such as NED, RL, and QB. Each task ($t_i : q^* \rightarrow q^+$) transforms a given representation q^* of a question q into another representation q^+. For example, NED and RL tasks transform the input representation *"What is the capital of Finland?"* into the representation *"What is the `dbo:capital` of `dbr:Finland`?"*. The entire set of QA components is denoted by $\mathcal{C} = \{C_1, C_2, \ldots, C_m\}$. Each component C_j solves one single QA task; $C_j^{t_i}$ corresponds to the QA task t_i in $\mathcal{T}$ implemented by C_j. For example, RNLIWOD implements the relation linking QA task, i.e. $RNLIWOD^{RL}$. Let $\rho(C_j)$ denote the performance of a QA component, then our key objective is to predict the likelihood of $\rho(C_j)$

[4]Component is similar to Relation Linker of https://github.com/dice-group/NLIWOD

[5]Component is based on https://github.com/dice-group/NLIWOD and (Unger et al., 2012).

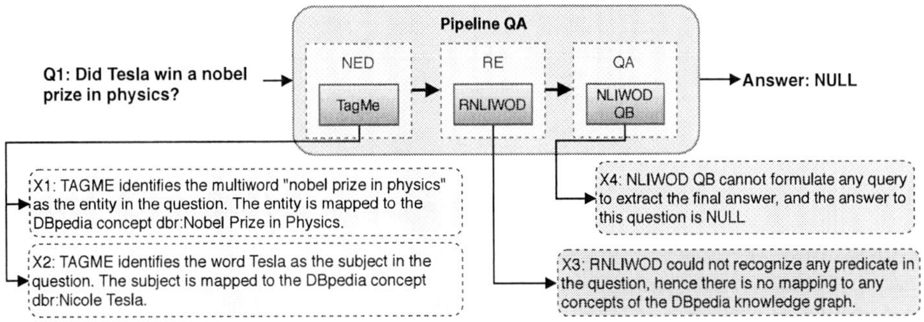

Figure 1: The QA pipeline generates the explanations in various stages of running; each explanation is generated per output of each integrated component. The demonstrated pipeline contains three components, i.e., NED, RL, and QB; the output(s) of each one is integrated into an explanation template and represented to the end user.

for a given representation q^* of q, a task t_i, and an underlying knowledge graph λ. This is denoted as $Pr(\rho(C_j)|q^*,t_i,\lambda)$. In this work, we assume a single knowledge graph (i.e. DBpedia); thus, λ is considered a constant parameter that does not impact the likelihood leading to:

$$Pr(\rho(C_j)|q^*,t_i) = Pr(\rho(C_j)|q^*,t_i,\lambda) \quad (1)$$

Further, we assume that the given representation q^* is equal to the initial input representation q for all the QA components, i.e. $q^* = q$.

Solution Suppose we are given a set of NL questions $\mathcal{Q}$ with the detailed results of performance for each component per task. We can then model the prediction goal $Pr(\rho(C_j)|q,t_i)$ as a supervised learning problem on a training set, i.e. a set of questions $\mathcal{Q}$ and a set of labels $\mathcal{L}$ representing the performance of C_j for a question q and a task t_i. In other words, for each individual task t_i and component C_j, the purpose is to train a supervised model that predicts the performance of the given component C_j for a given question q and task t_i leveraging the training set. If $|\mathcal{T}| = n$ and each task is performed by m components, and the QA pipeline integrates all the $n \times m$ components, then $n \times m$ individual learning models have to be built up.

Question Features. Since the input question q has a textual representation, it is necessary to automatically extract suitable features, i.e. $\mathcal{F}(q) = (f_1,\ldots,f_r)$. In order to obtain an abstract and concrete representation of NL questions, we reused question features proposed by (Singh et al., 2018b, 2019) which impact the performance of the QA systems. These features are: question length, answer type (list, number, boolean), Wh-word (who,what,which,etc.), and POS tags present in a question. Please note, our contribution is not the underlying Frankenstein framework, we reused it for the completion of the approach. Our contribution is to add valid explanation to each step of the QA pipeline, and empirical study to support our hypothesis.

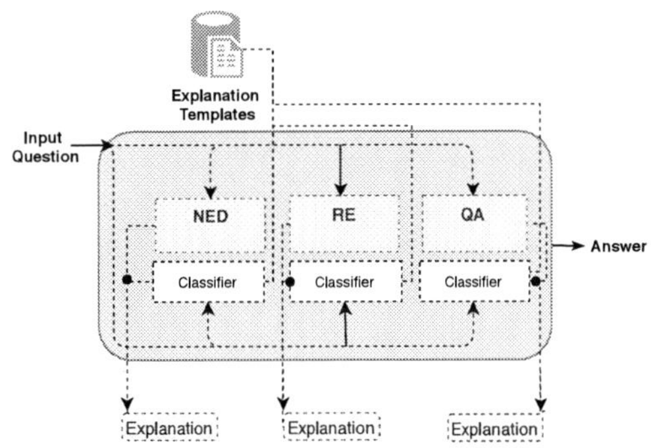

Figure 2: This figure sketches a top overview of our approach. There is a classifier for each component, which predicts the output of the associated component. Also, there is a repository of the explanation templates. Thus, based on the prediction of the classifier and the actual output of the component, a suitable template is filtered. For final explanation, the output of the component was incorporated into the template.

4.2 Methodology

Figure 2 shows the architecture of our approach. Initially, a pipeline for a QA system is built up; in our case we used Frankenstein platform (Singh et al., 2018b,a) to facilitate building up a pipeline. Please note, we do not aim to build a new QA system and reused an existing implementation. We extend the Frankenstein QA pipeline as illustrated in Figure 2. We rely on the best performing pipeline reported in (Singh et al., 2018b) over LC-QuAD dataset

(Trivedi et al., 2017). In addition, we manually populated a repository of explanation templates. For example, all the required explanation templates for NED components are created for cases such as templates for wrong answers, when components produce no answer, and in the case of correct answers. Similarly, the templates for other tasks such as RE an QB were handcrafted. Please note that these templates are generic, thereby they do not depend on the employed component. For example, if we integrate another NED component rather than TagMe, there is no need to update the template repositories. In the next step, we trained classifiers based on the settings which will be presented in the next section. Thus, when a new question arrives at the pipeline, in addition to running the pipeline to exploit the answer, our trained classifiers are also executed. Then the predictions of the classifiers lead us to choose appropriate templates from the repositories. The filtered templates incorporate the output of the components to produce salient representations for NL explanations. The flow of the explanations is represented to the end user besides the final answer.

Templates for Explanation To support our approach for explainable QA, we handcrafted 11 different templates for the explanation. We create placeholders in the predefined templates to verbalize the output of the QA components. Consider the explanation provided in Figure 1. The original template for explaining the output of TagMe component is: `TagMe identifies the multiword` **`X`** `as the entity in the question. The entity is mapped to the DBpedia concept` **`dbr:W`**`.` The placeholders **X** and **dbr:W** are replaced accordingly for each question if a classifier selects this template in its prediction.

5 Experimental Study

We direct our experiment in response to our two research questions (*i.e.,* RQ1 and RQ2) respectively. First, we pursue the following question *"How effective is our approach for generating explanations?"* This evaluation implies the demonstration of the success of our approach in generating proper explanations. It quantitatively evaluates the effectiveness of our approach. On the contrary, the second discourse of the experiment is an HCI study in response to the question *"How effective is the perception of the end user on our explanations?"* This experiment qualitatively evaluates user perception based on the human factors introduced earlier (cf. Section 1). In the following Subsections, we detail our experimental setups, achieved results, and insights over the outcomes of the evaluation.

5.1 Quantitative Evaluation

This experiment is concerned with the question *"How effective is our approach for generating explanations?"*. We measure the effectiveness in terms of the preciseness of the explanations. Regarding the architecture of our approach, choosing the right explanation template depends on the prediction of the classifiers. If classifiers precisely predict a correct output for the underlying components, then consequently, the right templates will be chosen.

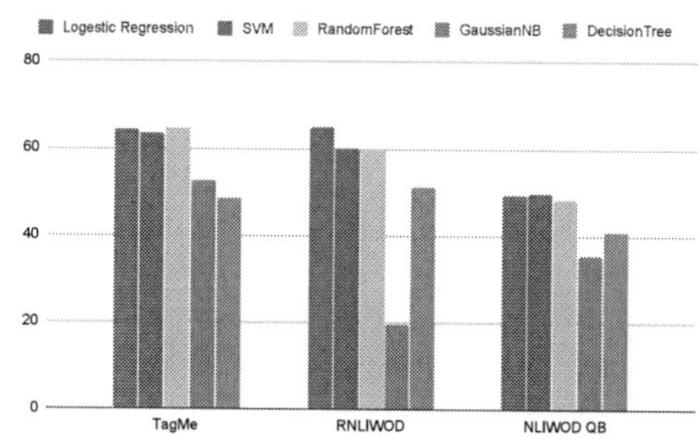

Figure 3: This figure illustrates the accuracy of five classifiers per QA component: TagMe, RNLIWOD, and NLIWOD QB. Logistic Regression classifier performs best for all the components.

In other words, any flaw in the prediction leads to a wrong template. Thus, here we present the accuracy of our classifiers per component. We consider three generic classes, namely $O_c = \{Success, NoAnswer, WrongAnswer\}$ (cf. section 4) for the outputs of individual components. A benchmarking approach has been followed to choose best classifier per task. We employ five different classifiers (SVM, Logistic Regression, Random Forest, Gaussian NB, and Decision Tree) and calculated each classifier's accuracy per component. To train the classifiers per component, we require to create a single dataset. The sample-set in training is formed by considering questions of the LC-QuAD dataset. To get the concrete representation of each question, we extracted the following features: question length, headword(who, what, how), answer types (boolean, number, list), and POS tags. If a particular feature is present, we consider the value 1; if not, then the value of that feature is 0 while representing the question. The label set of the training datasets for a given component was set up by measuring the micro F-Score of every given question for 3,253 questions from the LC-QuAD dataset. The F-score per question is calculated by adopting the same methodology proposed by (Singh et al., 2018b). We rely on 3,253 questions out of 5,000 questions of the LC-QuAD dataset because the gold standard SPARQL queries of the remaining 1,747 questions do not return any answer from DBpedia endpoint (also reported by (Azmy et al., 2018)). The classifier predicts if a component can answer the question or not, and trained using features extracted from the natural language questions against the F score per question. During the training phase, each classifier was tuned with a range of regularization on the dataset. We used the cross-validation approach with 10 folds on the LC-QuAD dataset. We employ a QA pipeline containing TagMe (Ferragina and Scaiella, 2010) for entity disambiguation, RNLIWOD[6] for relation linking, and NLIWOD QB[7] for SPARQL query builder. Figure 3 reports the accuracy of five classifiers (average of all classes). Furthermore, Table 2 reports the accuracy of the best classifier (Logistic Regression in our case) for each component.

Component	Accuracy
TagMe	0.64
RNLIWOD	0.60
NLIWOD WB	0.49

Table 2: **Accuracy of our multi-class classifier for predicting type of explanation for each component.**

Observations. We observe that the logistic regression classifier performs best for predicting the output of components. However, the accuracy of the classifier is low as depicted in the Table 2. (Singh et al., 2018b) report accuracy of *binary classifiers* for TagMe, RNLIWOD, and NLIWOD QB as 0.75, 0.72, and 0.65 respectively. When we train *multi-class classifiers* (*i.e.,* three classes) on the same dataset, we observe a drop in the accuracy. The main reason for the low performance of the classifiers is the low component accuracy (c.f. Table 1)

[6]Component is similar to Relation Linker of `https://github.com/dice-group/NLIWOD`

[7]Component is based on `https://github.com/dice-group/NLIWOD` and (Unger et al., 2012).

5.2 User Perception Evaluation

In the second experiment, we pursue the following research question: *"How is the perception of end user about explanations along the human factor dimensions?"* To respond to this question, we conduct the following experiment:

Experimental Setup: We perform a user study to evaluate how the explanations impact user perception. We aim at understanding user's feedback on the following four parameters inspired by (Ehsan et al., 2019; Ehsan and ark Riedl, 2019): 1) `Adequate Justification`: Does a user feel the answer to a particular question is justified or provided with the reasoning behind inferences of the answer? 2) `Education`: Does the user feel educated about the answer generation process so that she may better understand the strengths and limitations of the QA system? 3) `User involvement`: Does the user feel involved in allowing the user to add her knowledge and inference skills to the complete decision process? 4) `Acceptance`: Do explanations lead to a greater acceptance of the QA system in future interactions? With respect to the above criteria, we created an online survey to collect user feedback. The survey embraces random ten questions from our underlying dataset from a variety of answer types such as questions with the correct answer, incorrect answer, no answer (for which classifiers predict correct templates). The first part of the survey displays the questions to the user without any explanation. In the second part, the same ten questions, coupled with the explanations generated by our approach, are displayed to the user. The participants of the survey are asked to rate each representation of question/answer based on the four human factor dimensions (i.e., acceptance, justification, user involvement, and education). The rating scale is based on the Likert scale, which allows the participants to express how much they agree or disagree with a given statement (1:strongly disagree – 5:strongly agree). We circulated the survey to several channels of the co-authors' network, such as a graduate class of Semantic Web course, research groups in the USA and Europe, along with scientific mailing lists. Collectively we received responses from 80 participants. Please note, the number of participants is at par with the other explainable studies such as (Ehsan et al., 2019).

Results and Insights. Figure 4 summarizes the ratings of our user study. We evaluate the user responses based on the four human factor dimensions: `Adequate Justification`, `Education`, `User involvement`, and `Acceptance`. The summary of ratings for each dimension was captured in one individual chart. The green bars show the feedback over questions with provided explanations, and on the contrary, red bars are aggregated over the question with no explanation. The x-axis shows the Likert scale. The Y-axis is the distribution of users over the Likert scale for each class independently- with explanation and without explanation. Overall it shows a positive trend towards the agreement with the following facts; the provided explanations helped users to understand the underlying process better, justify a particular answer, involve the user in the complete process, and increase the acceptability of the answers. The green bars are larger in positive ratings, such as strongly agree.

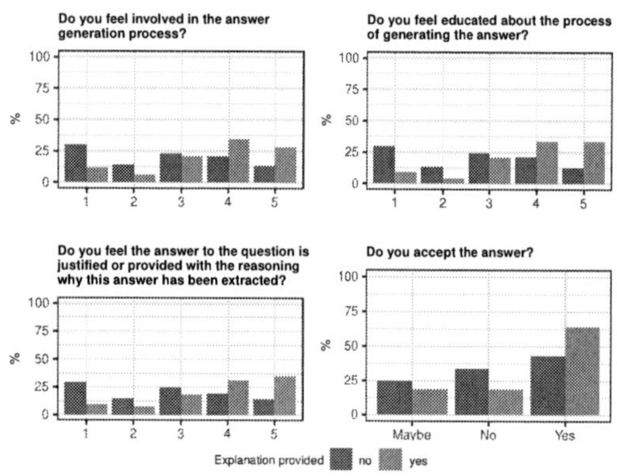

Figure 4: User perception Evaluation. The figure illustrates the comparative analysis of providing with and without explanation to the user. We consider the mean of all the responses. X-axis depicts the Likert scale (1 is strongly disagree, 5 is strongly agree). A clear trend in user responses shows that across all four parameters, there are many answers towards disagreement or neutral when no explanation is provided. In the case of explanation, users feel involved, and responses are shifted towards the agreement. Furthermore, users show more trust in the acceptance of the answer when provided with an explanation.

6 Discussion

In this paper, we focus on the challenge of explainable QA systems. We mainly target systems that consume data from the KGs. These systems receive a natural language question and then transform that to a formal query. Our primary aim is to take the initial steps to break down the full black-box QA systems. Thus, we reuse an existing QA pipeline systems since it already decompose the prominent tasks of the QA systems and then integrate individual implementations for each QA task. We based our approach and associated evaluation on the hypothesis that every component integrated into the pipeline should explain the output. It will educate and involve non-expert users and trigger them to trust and accept the system. Our findings in Section 5 support our hypothesis both on quantitative and qualitative evaluation. The limitation of our approach is that it heavily relies on the performance of the components. In the case of having low performing components, the accuracy of the classifiers is also downgraded. Although, on the one hand, this approach is shallow, one the other hand it avoids exposing the user to overwhelming details of the internal functionalities by showing succinct and user-friendly explanations. (Hoffman et al., 2017) noted that for improving the usability of XAI systems, it is essential to combine theories from social science and cognitive decision making to validate the intuition of what constitutes a "good explanation." Our work in this paper is limited to predefined template based explanations, and does not consider this aspect. Also, our work does not focus on the explainability of the behavior of the employed classifier, and the explanations only justify the final output of components.

7 Conclusion and Future Direction

In this paper, we proposed an approach that is automatic and supervised for generating explanations for a QA pipeline. Albeit simple, our approach intuitively expressive for the end user. This approach requires to train a classifier for every integrated component, which is costly in case the components are updated (new release) or replaced by a latest outperforming component. Our proposed approach induced in a QA pipeline of a modular framework is the first attempt for explainable QA systems over KGs. It paves the way for future contributions in developing explainable QA systems over KGs. Still, there are numerous rooms in this area that require the attention of the research community – for example, explanations regarding the quality of data, or metadata, or credibility of data publishers. Furthermore, recent attempts have been made to provide explanations of machine learning models (Guo et al., 2018). However, the inclusion of the explanations in neural approaches for question answering (such as in (Lukovnikov et al., 2017)) is still an open research question, and we plan to extend our work in this direction. The concerning domain of the system is also influential in explanations. for example, biomedical or marketing domains require various levels of details of explanations. In general, all of these concerns affect the acceptance and trust of the QA system by the end user. Our ambitious vision is to provide personalized and contextualized explanations, where the user feels more involved and educated.

References

Julia Angwin, Jeff Larson, Surya Mattu, and Lauren KirchnerIan Sample. 2016. Machine bias.

Sören Auer, Christian Bizer, Georgi Kobilarov, Jens Lehmann, Richard Cyganiak, and Zachary G. Ives. 2007. DBpedia: A Nucleus for a Web of Open Data. In *The Semantic Web, 6th International Semantic Web Conference, 2nd Asian Semantic Web Conference, ISWC 2007 + ASWC 2007, Busan, Korea, November 11-15, 2007.*

Michael Azmy, Peng Shi, Jimmy Lin, and Ihab Ilyas. 2018. Farewell freebase: Migrating the simplequestions dataset to dbpedia. In *Proceedings of the 27th International Conference on Computational Linguistics*, pages 2093–2103.

Jonathan Berant, Andrew Chou, Roy Frostig, and Percy Liang. 2013. Semantic Parsing on Freebase from Question-Answer Pairs. In *Proceedings of the 2013 Conference on Empirical Methods in Natural Language Processing, EMNLP 2013, 18-21 October 2013, Grand Hyatt Seattle, Seattle, Washington, USA, A meeting of SIGDAT, a Special Interest Group of the ACL*, pages 1533–1544.

Abhishek Bhandwaldar and Wlodek Zadrozny. 2018. Uncc qa: A biomedical question answering system. *EMNLP 2018*, page 66.

Julie Daher, Armelle Brun, and Anne Boyer. 2017. A review on explanations in recommender systems.

Dennis Diefenbach, Vanessa López, Kamal Deep Singh, and Pierre Maret. 2018. Core techniques of question answering systems over knowledge bases: a survey. *Knowledge and Information Systems*, 55(3):529–569.

Upol Ehsan and ark Riedl. 2019. On design and evaluation of human-centered explainable ai system. In *Human-Centered Machine Learning Perspectives Workshop at CHI.*

Upol Ehsan, Pradyumna Tambwekar, Larry Chan, Brent Harrison, and Mark O. Riedl. 2019. Automated rationale generation: a technique for explainable AI and its effects on human perceptions. In *Proceedings of the 24th International Conference on Intelligent User Interfaces, IUI 2019, Marina del Ray, CA, USA, March 17-20, 2019*, pages 263–274.

Paolo Ferragina and Ugo Scaiella. 2010. TAGME: on-the-fly annotation of short text fragments (by wikipedia entities). In *Proceedings of the 19th ACM Conference on Information and Knowledge Management, CIKM 2010, Toronto, Ontario, Canada, October 26-30, 2010*, pages 1625–1628.

John Fox, David Glasspool, Dan Grecu, Sanjay Modgil, Matthew South, and Vivek Patkar. 2007. Argumentation-based inference and decision making–a medical perspective. *IEEE intelligent systems*, 22(6):34–41.

Wenbo Guo, Sui Huang, Yunzhe Tao, Xinyu Xing, and Lin Lin. 2018. Explaining deep learning models–a bayesian non-parametric approach. In *Advances in Neural Information Processing Systems*, pages 4514–4524.

Bradley Hayes and Julie A Shah. 2017. Improving robot controller transparency through autonomous policy explanation. In *2017 12th ACM/IEEE International Conference on Human-Robot Interaction (HRI*, pages 303–312. IEEE.

Lisa Anne Hendricks, Zeynep Akata, Marcus Rohrbach, Jeff Donahue, Bernt Schiele, and Trevor Darrell. 2016. Generating visual explanations. In *European Conference on Computer Vision*, pages 3–19. Springer.

Jonathan L Herlocker, Joseph A Konstan, and John Riedl. 2000. Explaining collaborative filtering recommendations. In *Proceedings of the 2000 ACM conference on Computer supported cooperative work*, pages 241–250. ACM.

Robert R Hoffman, Shane T Mueller, and Gary Klein. 2017. Explaining explanation, part 2: empirical foundations. *IEEE Intelligent Systems*, 32(4):78–86.

Konrad Höffner, Sebastian Walter, Edgard Marx, Ricardo Usbeck, Jens Lehmann, and Axel-Cyrille Ngonga Ngomo. 2017. Survey on challenges of Question Answering in the Semantic Web. *Semantic Web.*

Dietmar Jannach, Markus Zanker, Alexander Felfernig, and Gerhard Friedrich. 2010. *Recommender systems: an introduction.* Cambridge University Press.

Zhen Jia, Abdalghani Abujabal, Rishiraj Saha Roy, Jannik Strötgen, and Gerhard Weikum. 2018. Tequila: Temporal question answering over knowledge bases. In *Proceedings of the 27th ACM International Conference on Information and Knowledge Management*, pages 1807–1810. ACM.

Jin-Dong Kim, Christina Unger, Axel-Cyrille Ngonga Ngomo, André Freitas, Young-gyun Hahm, Jiseong Kim, Sangha Nam, Gyu-Hyun Choi, Jeong-uk Kim, Ricardo Usbeck, et al. 2017. OKBQA Framework for collaboration on developing natural language question answering systems.

Pigi Kouki, James Schaffer, Jay Pujara, John O'Donovan, and Lise Getoor. 2017. User preferences for hybrid explanations. In *Proceedings of the Eleventh ACM Conference on Recommender Systems*, pages 84–88. ACM.

Todd Kulesza, Margaret Burnett, Weng-Keen Wong, and Simone Stumpf. 2015. Principles of explanatory debugging to personalize interactive machine learning. In *Proceedings of the 20th international conference on intelligent user interfaces*, pages 126–137. ACM.

Qing Li, Jianlong Fu, Dongfei Yu, Tao Mei, and Jiebo Luo. 2018. Tell-and-answer: Towards explainable visual question answering using attributes and captions. In *Proceedings of the 2018 Conference on Empirical Methods in Natural Language Processing*, pages 1338–1346.

Heguang Liu. 2019. Conditioning lstm decoder and bi-directional attention based question answering system. *arXiv preprint arXiv:1905.02019*.

Denis Lukovnikov, Asja Fischer, Jens Lehmann, and Sören Auer. 2017. Neural network-based question answering over knowledge graphs on word and character level. In *Proceedings of the 26th International Conference on World Wide Web, WWW 2017, Perth, Australia, April 3-7, 2017*, pages 1211–1220.

Tim Miller. 2018. Explanation in artificial intelligence: Insights from the social sciences. *Artificial Intelligence*.

Johanna D Moore and William R Swartout. 1988. Explanation in expert systems: A survey. Technical report, University of Southern California, USA.

Axel-Cyrille Ngonga Ngomo, Lorenz Bühmann, Christina Unger, Jens Lehmann, and Daniel Gerber. 2013. Sorry, i don't speak sparql: translating sparql queries into natural language. In *Proceedings of the 22nd international conference on World Wide Web*, pages 977–988. ACM.

Michael Petrochuk and Luke Zettlemoyer. 2018. Simplequestions nearly solved: A new upperbound and baseline approach. In *Proceedings of the 2018 Conference on Empirical Methods in Natural Language Processing*, pages 554–558.

Dharmen Punjani, K Singh, Andreas Both, Manolis Koubarakis, Ioannis Angelidis, Konstantina Bereta, Themis Beris, Dimitris Bilidas, T Ioannidis, Nikolaos Karalis, et al. 2018. Template-based question answering over linked geospatial data. In *Proceedings of the 12th Workshop on Geographic Information Retrieval*, page 7. ACM.

Marco Tulio Ribeiro, Sameer Singh, and Carlos Guestrin. 2016. Why should i trust you?: Explaining the predictions of any classifier. In *Proceedings of the 22nd ACM SIGKDD international conference on knowledge discovery and data mining*, pages 1135–1144. ACM.

Wojciech Samek, Thomas Wiegand, and Klaus-Robert Müller. 2017. Explainable artificial intelligence: Understanding, visualizing and interpreting deep learning models. *arXiv preprint arXiv:1708.08296*.

Saeedeh Shekarpour, Edgard Marx, Axel-Cyrille Ngonga Ngomo, and Sören Auer. 2015. SINA: semantic interpretation of user queries for question answering on interlinked data. *J. Web Semant.*, 30:39–51.

Saeedeh Shekarpour, Axel-Cyrille Ngonga Ngomo, and Sören Auer. 2013. Question answering on interlinked data. In *22nd International World Wide Web Conference, WWW '13, Rio de Janeiro, Brazil, May 13-17, 2013*, pages 1145–1156.

Edward H Shortliffe. 1974. A rule-based computer program for advising physicians regarding antimicrobial therapy selection. In *Proceedings of the 1974 annual ACM conference-Volume 2*, pages 739–739. ACM.

Kuldeep Singh. 2019. Towards dynamic composition of question answering pipelines. *Doctoral Thesis, University of Bonn, Germany*.

Kuldeep Singh, Andreas Both, Arun Sethupat Radhakrishna, and Saeedeh Shekarpour. 2018a. Frankenstein: A platform enabling reuse of question answering components. In *The Semantic Web - 15th International Conference, ESWC 2018, Heraklion, Crete, Greece, June 3-7, 2018, Proceedings*, pages 624–638.

Kuldeep Singh, Arun Sethupat Radhakrishna, Andreas Both, Saeedeh Shekarpour, Ioanna Lytra, Ricardo Usbeck, Akhilesh Vyas, Akmal Khikmatullaev, Dharmen Punjani, Christoph Lange, Maria-Esther Vidal, Jens Lehmann, and Sören Auer. 2018b. Why reinvent the wheel: Let's build question answering systems together. In *Proceedings of the 2018 World Wide Web Conference on World Wide Web, WWW 2018, Lyon, France, April 23-27, 2018*, pages 1247–1256.

Kuldeep Singh, Muhammad Saleem, Abhishek Nadgeri, Felix Conrads, Jeff Pan, Axel-Cyrille Ngonga Ngomo, and Jens Lehmann. 2019. Qaldgen: Towards microbenchmarking of question answering systems over knowledge graphs. In *ISWC*.

Kristen Stubbs, Pamela J Hinds, and David Wettergreen. 2007. Autonomy and common ground in human-robot interaction: A field study. *IEEE Intelligent Systems*, 22(2):42–50.

Priyansh Trivedi, Gaurav Maheshwari, Mohnish Dubey, and Jens Lehmann. 2017. LC-QuAD: A Corpus for Complex Question Answering over Knowledge Graphs. In *The Semantic Web - ISWC 2017 - 16th International Semantic Web Conference, Vienna, Austria, October 21-25, 2017, Proceedings, Part II*, pages 210–218. Springer.

Christina Unger, Lorenz Bühmann, Jens Lehmann, Axel-Cyrille Ngonga Ngomo, Daniel Gerber, and

Philipp Cimiano. 2012. Template-based question answering over RDF data. In *Proceedings of the 21st World Wide Web Conference 2012, WWW 2012, Lyon, France, April 16-20, 2012*, pages 639–648. ACM.

Christina Unger, Corina Forascu, Vanessa López, Axel-Cyrille Ngonga Ngomo, Elena Cabrio, Philipp Cimiano, and Sebastian Walter. 2015. Question Answering over Linked Data (QALD-5). In *Working Notes of CLEF 2015 - Conference and Labs of the Evaluation forum, Toulouse, France, September 8-11, 2015*. CEUR-WS.org.

Ricardo Usbeck, Axel-Cyrille Ngonga Ngomo, Lorenz Bühmann, and Christina Unger. 2015. Hawk–hybrid question answering using linked data. In *European Semantic Web Conference*, pages 353–368. Springer.

Jialin Wu and Raymond J Mooney. 2018. Faithful multimodal explanation for visual question answering. *arXiv preprint arXiv:1809.02805*.

Wei Yang, Yuqing Xie, Aileen Lin, Xingyu Li, Luchen Tan, Kun Xiong, Ming Li, and Jimmy Lin. 2019. End-to-end open-domain question answering with bertserini. *NAACL HLT 2019*, page 72.

Uncertainty and Traffic-Aware Active Learning for Semantic Parsing

Priyanka Sen
Amazon Alexa
sepriyan@amazon.com

Emine Yilmaz
Amazon Alexa
eminey@amazon.com

Abstract

Collecting training data for semantic parsing is a time-consuming and expensive task. As a result, there is growing interest in industry to reduce the number of annotations required to train a semantic parser, both to cut down on costs and to limit customer data handled by annotators. In this paper, we propose *uncertainty and traffic-aware active learning*, a novel active learning method that uses model confidence and utterance frequencies from customer traffic to select utterances for annotation. We show that our method significantly outperforms baselines on an internal customer dataset and the Facebook Task Oriented Parsing (TOP) dataset. On our internal dataset, our method achieves the same accuracy as random sampling with 2,000 fewer annotations.

1 Introduction

Semantic parsing is the task of mapping natural language to a machine-executable meaning representation. Supervised semantic parsing models are trained on corpora of natural language utterances with annotated meaning representations. Collecting these annotations is an expensive manual process, usually requiring expert annotators who are familiar with both the domain of utterances and the target meaning representation language (e.g. SQL).

Active learning is a method for collecting training data when annotating is difficult or budgets are limited (Settles, 2009). In active learning, an algorithm selects examples from an unlabeled set that are predicted to be more useful for the model if labeled. These examples are annotated and the model is retrained in an iterative process. The goal of an active learner is to reach higher performance faster than a random sampling baseline.

In this paper, we propose *uncertainty and traffic-aware active learning*, a simple yet effective method to improve a semantic parser. In our setup, we assume access to a set of initially annotated utterances and a large set of unlabeled utterances from customer traffic. We show that by using a combination of uncertainty and utterance frequency from traffic, we can achieve significantly higher performance than baselines on both an internal customer dataset and on the Facebook Task Oriented Parsing (TOP) dataset (Gupta et al., 2018).

2 Related Work

Active learning has been applied to various NLP tasks (Zhou et al., 2010; Li et al., 2012; Shen et al., 2017; Peshterliev et al., 2019; Chen et al., 2019). Duong et al. (2018) presented one of the first works on active learning for deep semantic parsing and found that selecting low-confidence examples outperformed random examples on two datasets but failed on a third. Koshorek et al. (2019) experimented with learning to actively-learn for semantic parsing, a method where the active learner is a learned model, but failed to see better performance than random sampling. Ni et al. (2020) proposed a framework where a weakly trained semantic parser was allowed to actively select examples for extra supervision. The authors found that selecting the least confident of the incorrect examples led to the best performance. Incorrect examples were identified by executing the predicted query and comparing the predicted answer with an expected answer. In this paper, we experiment with using uncertainty and utterance frequencies from customer traffic, a feature often found in industry logs.

3 Uncertainty and Traffic-Aware Active Learning

We propose *uncertainty and traffic-aware active learning* for semantic parsing. Our method is inspired by Mehrotra and Yilmaz (2015), who presented an active learning method for ranking al-

Proceedings of the First Workshop on Interactive and Executable Semantic Parsing, pages 12–17

https://doi.org/10.18653/v1/P17

gorithms which selects examples that are both informative to the model and representative of the dataset. The authors found that including a representativeness measure helped offset the tendency of informativeness measures to select outliers. In their paper, the authors measured informativeness as permutation probability based on a committee of ranking models, so a query where the most certain committee member had the least confidence was considered more informative. For representativeness, the authors used an LDA model to create a feature vector for each query. If a query's feature vector had higher cosine similarity to the average feature vector of all queries, the query was considered more representative.

In our method, we also use informativeness and representativeness, but we introduce new ways to measure both that can be applied to semantic parsing tasks. For each utterance *u* in a set of unlabeled utterances *U*, we calculate f(*u*), a sampling weight associated with *u*, as:

$$f(u) = \beta \frac{\phi(u)}{\sum\limits_{u \in U} \phi(u)} + (1-\beta) \frac{\psi(u)}{\sum\limits_{u \in U} \psi(u)} \qquad (1)$$

where $\phi(u)$ is the representativeness and $\psi(u)$ is the informativeness of *u*. We measure $\phi(u)$ as the utterance frequency, calculated as the number of times the utterance *u* appeared during a given time window of traffic. We measure $\psi(u)$ as 1 - our model's confidence on *u*. To calculate confidence, we use perplexity per word, which is the inverse probability of a model's output normalized by the number of words. We convert this perplexity into a confidence score by scaling it to a value between [0,1] using the function in Algorithm 1. The threshold is set to 0.9, which was fine-tuned based on the model's accuracy in production. In this function, confidence approaches 1 as perplexity approaches 0, confidence is 0.5 when perplexity is the threshold, and confidence approaches 0 as perplexity approaches infinity. While this scaled perplexity is not an exact measure of confidence, we found that it was effective in our experiments.

Both $\phi(u)$ and $\psi(u)$ are normalized by the sum of all values of $\phi(u)$ and $\psi(u)$. We use f(*u*) as a weight on each utterance when sampling. Utterances that maximize f(*u*) by having higher frequencies and lower confidences are more likely to be selected.

The β is a fine-tunable term that weighs the utterance frequency against the confidence. We manually fine-tuned β by training 9 models with different values ranging from 0.1 to 0.9 and compared performance in terms of exact-match accuracy. We found that a β of 0.4 performed the best on our internal dataset and a β of 0.5 performed the best on TOP, and so we use these β values in this paper.

Algorithm 1: Perplexity to confidence

```
p ← perplexity
if p > threshold: then
  | return 1 / (2 + (100 * (p - threshold)));
else
  | return 1 - 0.5 * (p / threshold);
end
```

3.1 Semantic Parsing Model

The semantic parsing model we use to evaluate our method is a reimplementation of the sequence-to-sequence model with pointer generator network proposed by Rongali et al. (2020), which achieved state-of-the-art performance on Facebook TOP (Gupta et al., 2018). We use a BERT-Base model (Devlin et al., 2019) as the encoder and a transformer based on Vaswani et al. (2017) as the decoder. The encoder converts a sequence of words into a sequence of embeddings. Then at each time step, the decoder outputs either a symbol from the output vocabulary or a pointer to an input token. A final softmax layer provides a probability distribution over all actions, and beam search maximizes the output sequence probability.

3.2 Compared Approaches

We compare our method to the following baselines.

RANDOM: Our random baseline randomly samples utterances for annotation.

TRAFFIC-AWARE: Our traffic-aware baseline uses utterance frequencies as a weight on each utterance, prioritizing utterances asked more often. In datasets containing duplicates, this is equivalent to random sampling.

CLUSTERING: In our clustering baseline (Kang et al., 2004; Ni et al., 2020), we compute a RoBERTa (Liu et al., 2019) embedding using sentence-transformers[1] for each utterance. We cluster the embeddings with

[1]https://github.com/UKPLab/sentence-transformers

	Internal	TOP
Train	10,000	500
Dev	2,000	4,032
Test	5,000	8,241
Unlabeled	100,000	13,680
Src Vocab	30,160	11,873
Tgt Vocab	5,400	116

Table 1: Details of the datasets. *Train* is the starting training set in our experiments. *Unlabeled* is the set from which additional training examples are sampled.

Internal	what is the capital of france, `is_the_capital_of(@ptr5)`
TOP	Any accidents along Culver, `[IN:GET_INFO_TRAFFIC @ptr0 @ptr1 @ptr2 [SL:LOCATION @ptr3]]`

Table 2: Examples from the datasets. `@ptrs` are pointers to a source token. In the first example `@ptr5` refers to the 5th token in the source, "france".

k-means and set the number of clusters to the round's budget (i.e. if our budget is 500 utterances, we create 500 clusters). Then we randomly sample 1 example per cluster.

LEAST CONFIDENCE: Our least confidence baseline (Lewis and Catlett, 1994; Culotta and McCallum, 2005) selects utterances with the lowest model confidence.

MARGIN OF CONFIDENCE: Our margin of confidence baseline (Settles and Craven, 2008) calculates the difference in confidence between the top two predictions in an n-best list. Large differences between the top two predictions indicate there is a clear top prediction, while small differences indicate greater model uncertainty. We select the examples with the smallest difference in confidence.

UNCERTAINTY-AWARE: A less deterministic version of Least Confidence. We use 1 - model confidence as a weight on each utterance, prioritizing utterances with low confidence.

UNCERTAINTY + CORRECTNESS: Our uncertainty + correctness baseline (Ni et al., 2020) selects the most uncertain of the predictions that are incorrect. In practice, there are several ways to identify an incorrect prediction, such as checking if 1) a query fails to execute, 2) a query executes but fails to answer, or 3) a query executes but does not return the expected answer. In our experimental setup, we use a more favorable setting by checking the prediction against the expected representation.

4 Datasets

We run experiments on both an internal customer dataset and the Facebook Task Oriented Parsing (TOP) dataset (Gupta et al., 2018). Details and examples are shown in Tables 1 and 2.

Our internal dataset contains open-domain factual questions asked by customers to a commercial voice assistant. The utterances are anonymized and labeled with a meaning representation by an internal high-precision rule-based system. We also calculate a count for each utterance based on how often the utterance was asked in a given period of time. This dataset contains only unique utterances, which prevents selecting the same utterance multiple times for annotation.

To our knowledge, there is no public semantic parsing dataset with question frequencies, and so we use a modified version of TOP. TOP is a semantic parsing dataset of 45k crowdsourced queries about navigation and public events. These queries are manually labeled with a meaning representation. In order to create a measure of representativeness, we assume that utterances with an exact-matched meaning representation are semantically similar. Utterances with meaning representations that appear more often are considered more representative. We keep one utterance per exact-matched meaning representation, and use the counts as a measure of how popular this type of question is among users. This is done for experimental purposes. In a real setting without the labels, we could use alternate measures of semantic similarity to identify more popular questions.

5 Experiments

For controlled experimentation, we simulate active learning by treating a subset of our data as unlabeled. When an unlabeled example is selected, we reveal the label and add it to the training set. All our experiments are run on an Nvidia Tesla v100 16GB GPU and the results are reported as exact match accuracy.

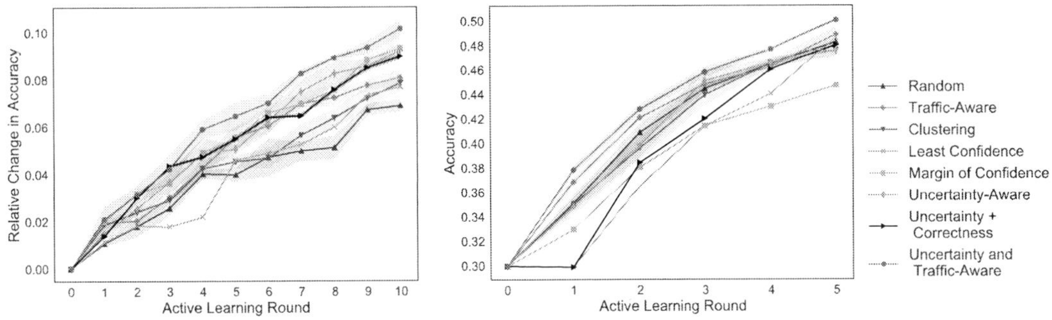

(a) Internal (b) TOP

Figure 1: Results of the experiments. Scores are calculated as exact-match accuracy. We only report relative change in accuracy for the internal dataset. The shaded regions represent the standard error for each point.

5.1 Internal Dataset

For our internal dataset, we start with a base training set of 10,000 utterances and set an annotation budget of 5,000 utterances. In each round, we sample 500 utterances from the unlabeled set, append them with their labels to the training set, and fully retrain the model. We repeat this for 10 rounds and report results as an average over 5 runs.

The results are shown in terms of relative change in exact-match accuracy in Figure 1a. Our method initially has similar performance to uncertainty-based baselines, but after Round 4, our method outperforms all the baselines. Table 3 has results of paired t-tests comparing our method to each baseline. All the p-values are <0.05, showing statistical significance. In particular, our method outperforms random sampling. The examples picked by the first 6 rounds of uncertainty and traffic-aware sampling (accuracy $\Delta 7.0\%$ at round 6) are as valuable as the examples picked by all 10 rounds of random sampling (accuracy $\Delta 6.9\%$ at round 10), saving on the cost of 2,000 annotations.

To better understand these results, we inspected examples selected by each method. We found that although the traffic-aware method picked popular utterances, annotating many similar questions had limited gains over time. On the other hand, uncertainty-based approaches picked more diverse examples, but since customer datasets can be noisy, they were prone to picking outliers that were not as useful to the model when annotated. By combining frequency with uncertainty, our method was able to prioritize popular but under-represented examples, which were both interesting for customers and interesting for the model, and this gave us the best performance.

Baseline	Internal	TOP
Random	$p<.001$	$p=.01$
Traffic-Aware	$p<.001$	$p=.008$
Clustering	$p<.001$	$p=.01$
Least Confidence	$p<.001$	$p=.02$
Margin of Confidence	$p=.002$	$p=.004$
Uncertainty-Aware	$p<.001$	$p=.02$
Uncertainty + Correctness	$p=.001$	$p=.03$

Table 3: Results of paired t-tests comparing our method to each baseline. $p<.05$ is considered significant

5.2 TOP

We next ran experiments on TOP. Given that TOP is a smaller and simpler dataset (e.g. target vocab of 116 vs. 5,400), we start with a smaller base training set of 500 examples and set an annotation budget of 500 examples. In each round, we sample 100 examples from the unlabeled set, append them with their labels to the training set, and fully retrain the model. We see the effect of our method as early as Round 1, so we stop after 5 rounds and report results as an average over 5 runs.

The results are shown as exact-match accuracy in Figure 1b and the p-values from paired t-tests are in Table 3. These results again show that our method significantly outperforms the baselines. Even though the traffic weights in TOP are not from customer traffic, traffic-aware sampling performs almost as well as our method. This suggests that MRL frequency is a helpful measure for this test set. We also observe that some of our uncertainty-based baselines perform worse than random sampling, in contrast to our results on the internal dataset. We hypothesize this could be because uncertainty is a less useful signal from models built with smaller training sets (TOP: 500-1,000 training examples vs. Internal: 10,000-15,000 training examples) or because low confidence examples were less useful for TOP's test set. Uncertainty still provides some advantage, however, as the combination with MRL frequency leads to the best performance.

6 Conclusion

In this work, we present *uncertainty and traffic-aware active learning*, a method that uses model confidence and traffic frequency to improve a semantic parsing model. We show that our method significantly outperforms baselines on both an internal dataset and TOP. Our method achieves the same precision as random sampling with 2,000 fewer annotations on our internal dataset. Based on our results, we present our method as a way to improve semantic parsers while reducing annotation costs and limiting customer data shown to annotators.

References

Xi C. Chen, Adithya Sagar, Justine T. Kao, Tony Y. Li, Christopher Klein, Stephen Pulman, Ashish Garg, and Jason D. Williams. 2019. Active Learning for Domain Classification in a Commercial Spoken Personal Assistant. In *Proc. Interspeech 2019*, pages 1478–1482.

Aron Culotta and Andrew McCallum. 2005. Reducing labeling effort for structured prediction tasks. In *AAAI*, volume 5, pages 746–751.

Jacob Devlin, Ming-Wei Chang, Kenton Lee, and Kristina Toutanova. 2019. BERT: Pre-training of deep bidirectional transformers for language understanding. In *Proceedings of the 2019 Conference of the North American Chapter of the Association for Computational Linguistics: Human Language Technologies, Volume 1 (Long and Short Papers)*, pages 4171–4186, Minneapolis, Minnesota. Association for Computational Linguistics.

Long Duong, Hadi Afshar, Dominique Estival, Glen Pink, Philip Cohen, and Mark Johnson. 2018. Active learning for deep semantic parsing. In *Proceedings of the 56th Annual Meeting of the Association for Computational Linguistics (Volume 2: Short Papers)*, pages 43–48, Melbourne, Australia. Association for Computational Linguistics.

Sonal Gupta, Rushin Shah, Mrinal Mohit, Anuj Kumar, and Mike Lewis. 2018. Semantic parsing for task oriented dialog using hierarchical representations. In *Proceedings of the 2018 Conference on Empirical Methods in Natural Language Processing*, pages 2787–2792, Brussels, Belgium. Association for Computational Linguistics.

Jaeho Kang, Kwang Ryel Ryu, and Hyuk-Chul Kwon. 2004. Using cluster-based sampling to select initial training set for active learning in text classification. In *Pacific-Asia conference on knowledge discovery and data mining*, pages 384–388. Springer.

Omri Koshorek, Gabriel Stanovsky, Yichu Zhou, Vivek Srikumar, and Jonathan Berant. 2019. On the limits of learning to actively learn semantic representations. In *Proceedings of the 23rd Conference on Computational Natural Language Learning (CoNLL)*, pages 452–462, Hong Kong, China. Association for Computational Linguistics.

David D Lewis and Jason Catlett. 1994. Heterogeneous uncertainty sampling for supervised learning. In *Machine Learning Proceedings 1994*, pages 148–156. Elsevier.

Shoushan Li, Shengfeng Ju, Guodong Zhou, and Xiaojun Li. 2012. Active learning for imbalanced sentiment classification. In *Proceedings of the 2012 Joint Conference on Empirical Methods in Natural Language Processing and Computational Natural Language Learning*, pages 139–148, Jeju Island, Korea. Association for Computational Linguistics.

Yinhan Liu, Myle Ott, Naman Goyal, Jingfei Du, Mandar Joshi, Danqi Chen, Omer Levy, Mike Lewis, Luke Zettlemoyer, and Veselin Stoyanov. 2019. RoBERTa: A robustly optimized BERT pretraining approach. *arXiv preprint arXiv:1907.11692*.

Rishabh Mehrotra and Emine Yilmaz. 2015. Representative & informative query selection for learning to rank using submodular functions. In *Proceedings of the 38th International ACM SIGIR Conference on Research and Development in Information Retrieval*, SIGIR '15, page 545–554, New York, NY, USA. Association for Computing Machinery.

Ansong Ni, Pengcheng Yin, and Graham Neubig. 2020. Merging weak and active supervision for semantic parsing. In *Thirty-Fourth AAAI Conference on Artificial Intelligence (AAAI)*, New York, USA.

Stanislav Peshterliev, John Kearney, Abhyuday Jagannatha, Imre Kiss, and Spyros Matsoukas. 2019. Active learning for new domains in natural language understanding. In *Proceedings of the 2019 Conference of the North American Chapter of the Association for Computational Linguistics: Human Language Technologies, Volume 2 (Industry Papers)*, pages 90–96, Minneapolis, Minnesota. Association for Computational Linguistics.

Subendhu Rongali, Luca Soldaini, Emilio Monti, and Wael Hamza. 2020. Don't parse, generate! A sequence to sequence architecture for task-oriented semantic parsing. In *Proceedings of The Web Conference 2020*, pages 2962–2968.

Burr Settles. 2009. Active learning literature survey. Technical report, University of Wisconsin-Madison Department of Computer Sciences.

Burr Settles and Mark Craven. 2008. An analysis of active learning strategies for sequence labeling tasks. In *Proceedings of the 2008 Conference on Empirical Methods in Natural Language Processing*, pages 1070–1079.

Yanyao Shen, Hyokun Yun, Zachary Lipton, Yakov Kronrod, and Animashree Anandkumar. 2017. Deep active learning for named entity recognition. In *Proceedings of the 2nd Workshop on Representation Learning for NLP*, pages 252–256, Vancouver, Canada. Association for Computational Linguistics.

Ashish Vaswani, Noam Shazeer, Niki Parmar, Jakob Uszkoreit, Llion Jones, Aidan N Gomez, Ł ukasz Kaiser, and Illia Polosukhin. 2017. Attention is all you need. In I. Guyon, U. V. Luxburg, S. Bengio, H. Wallach, R. Fergus, S. Vishwanathan, and R. Garnett, editors, *Advances in Neural Information Processing Systems 30*, pages 5998–6008. Curran Associates, Inc.

Shusen Zhou, Qingcai Chen, and Xiaolong Wang. 2010. Active deep networks for semi-supervised sentiment classification. In *COLING 2010: Posters*, pages 1515–1523, Beijing, China. COLING 2010 Organizing Committee.

Improving Sequence-to-Sequence Semantic Parser for Task Oriented Dialog

Chaoting Xuan
VMware
cxuan@vmware.com

Abstract

Task Oriented Parsing (TOP) attempts to map utterances to compositional requests, including multiple intents and their slots. Previous work focus on a tree-based hierarchical meaning representation, and applying constituency parsing techniques to address TOP. In this paper, we propose a new format of meaning representation that is more compact and amenable to sequence-to-sequence (seq-to-seq) models. A simple copy-augmented seq-to-seq parser is built and evaluated over a public TOP dataset, resulting in 3.44% improvement over prior best seq-to-seq parser (exact match accuracy), which is also comparable to constituency parsers' performance[1].

1 Introduction

Today, most virtual assistants like Alexa and Siri are task oriented dialog systems based on GUS architecture (Bobrow et al. 1977; Jurafsky and Martin. 2019). They parse users' utterances to semantic frames composed of intents and slots. An intent normally represents a web API call to some downstream domain application to fulfill certain task. Slots correspond to parameters required in web API calls. In this paper, the task of parsing utterances to semantic frames is called Task Oriented Parsing (TOP).

Many prior work (Liu and Lane, 2016; Goyal et al. 2018) concentrate on parsing single-intent requests in which one utterance contains only one intent and its slots. Shah et al. (2018) proposes a hierarchical TOP representation to model the nested requests: one utterance contains multiple recursive intents and their slots. Figure 1.a shows an example of the hierarchical TOP representation, which is called *base representation* in this paper. Other than expressiveness, base representation also enjoys the easy annotation, efficient parsing and low adoption barrier in practice. Two types of models have been employed to perform TOP tasks: seq-to-seq models, and constituency parsing models (Dyer et al., 2016; Gaddy et al. 2018). It has been reported that the latter consistently outperforms the former, probably because constituency parsing algorithms are dedicated to serving tree-based representation by design, while seq-to-seq architecture are purposed to serve more generalized form of representations such as graph and logical form (Dong and Lapata, 2016; Jia and Liang 2016).

In this paper we introduce a compact TOP representation, which has fewer tokens than base presentation. Further, we build a simple seq-to-seq model with attention-based copy mechanism to evaluate the effectiveness of the compact representation. Experimental results on a public TOP dataset show that this approach can significantly improve seq-to-seq parser's inference performance and close its gap to current constituency parsers, who cannot handle the new TOP representation.

2 Related Work

Shah et al. (2018) proposes the hierarchical TOP representation and uses RNNG (Dyer et al., 2016), a standard transition-based constituency parsing algorithm, to build a TOP parser, which outperforms the baseline seq-to-seq parsers by 2.64%. Einolghozati et al. (2018) further optimizes the RNNG parser using ensembling, contextual word embedding and language model re-ranking, leading to higher exact match accuracy. However, training a RNNG model is expensive and almost one-scale slower than training a seq-to-seq model. Later, Pasupat et al. (2019) presents a chart-based (constituency) TOP parser, and it can reach fast training and high inference accuracy simultaneously.

3 Representation

In base representation, words are terminals, and intents and slots are nonterminals. The root node is an intent, and an intent is allowed to be nested inside a slot. In addition, base representation

1. *Source code is available at https://github.com/cxuan2019/Top*

Proceedings of the First Workshop on Interactive and Executable Semantic Parsing, pages 18–22
Online, November 19, 2020. ©2020 Association for Computational Linguistics
https://doi.org/10.18653/v1/P17

follows three constraints: 1. The top-level node must be an intent, 2. An intent can have words and/or slots as children, 3. A slot can have either words or an intent as children.

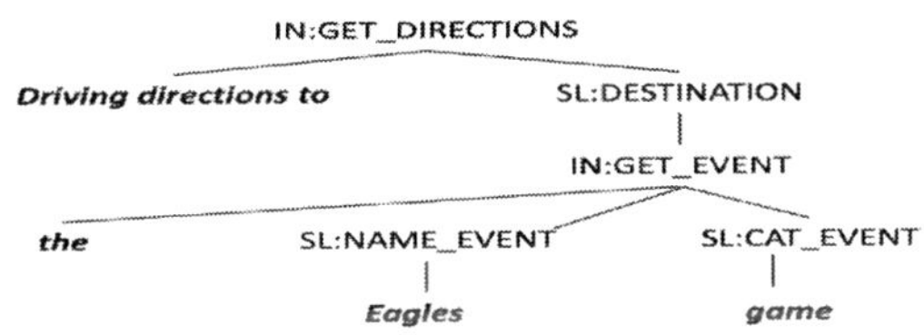

Fig 1.a: Base Representation. Intents are prefixed with IN: and slots with SL:.

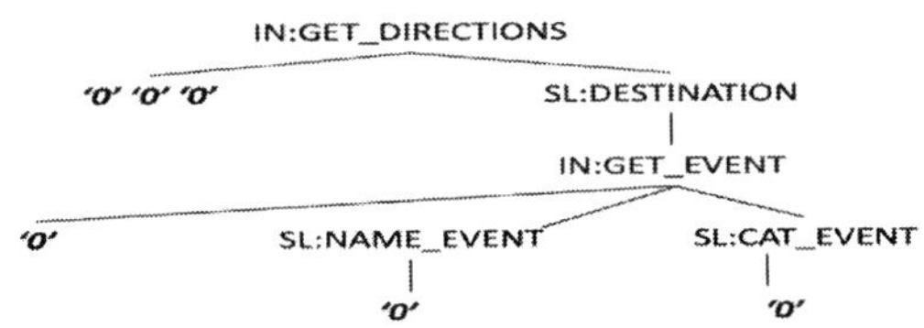

Fig 1.b: LOTV Representation. All words are replaced with token '0'.

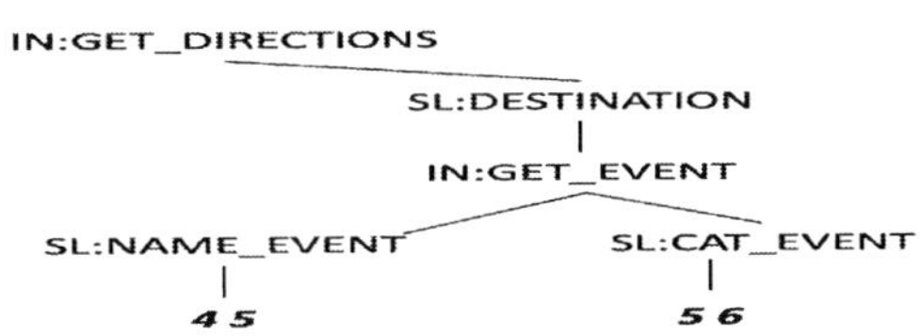

Fig 1.c: Compact Representation. Words are either gone or replaced with word indexes.

To simply seq-to-seq models, a single special token is used to replace multiple words in parses, which is called Limited Output Token Vocabulary (LOTV) representation (Shah et al., 2018). In the Figure 1.b, the special token used in LOTV representation is '0'. After using LOTV representation to substitute base representation, seq-to-seq model performs much better: almost 7% increase.

Compact representation is based on two observations: 1. Direct child tokens under an intent node are unnecessary to final execution of API calls; 2. A span of continuous words in the leaf of base representation can be encoded as a pair of positional indexes of starting word and ending word in source utterance. Specifically, compact representation is defined as a tree: root node is an intent; an intent node has either child slot nodes or no child node; a slot node has one child: either an intent node or a pair of word indexes that encode a continuous word span. Figure 1.c shows an example of compact representation.

Apparently, compact representation has fewer tokens than base representation and LOTV presentation. Its Vocabulary size is smaller than base representation, but bigger than LOTV representation.

4 Data

The TOP dataset[2] is introduced in the work of Shah et al. (2018), and it covers two domains: navigation and events. The utterances contain three types of queries: navigation, events and navigation to events. There are total 44783 annotated utterances with 25 intents and 36 slots. Each utterance is annotated with a hierarchical meaning representation. About 30% of records have nested requests. Among these data, the median depth of the trees is 2.54, and median length of the utterances is 8.93 tokens.

In this work, we remove the records that have IN:UNSUPPORTED intent from the dataset. After this, the dataset has 28414 training records, 4032 validation records and 8241 test records, identical to (Pasupat et al., 2019). Original dataset uses base representation, and we convert them to LOTV representation and compact representation. Average token lengths of LOTV and compact representations are 17 and 12; their vocabulary sizes are 60 and 93 respectively. Table 1 presents more statistics about the final dataset.

5 Model

We use a simple seq-to-seq with attention neural architecture to frame the TOP problem. Encoder is one-layer bi-directional recurrent neural network with LSTM (Hochreiter and Schmidhuber, 1997). The final output hidden states of both directions are concatenated and projected to the first input state of decoder through a linear layer. In decoder, attention and output token at time step t are computed as below:

$$z_t = [embed(y_{t-1});\ o_{t-1}] \tag{1}$$
$$h^{dec}, c^{dec} = LSTM(z_t, h^{dec}_{t-1}, c^{dec}_{t-1}) \tag{2}$$
$$e_t = (h^{dec}_t)^T W_{attProj} h^{enc} \tag{3}$$
$$\alpha_t = Softmax(e_t) \tag{4}$$
$$a_t = \textstyle\sum_i^m \alpha_{t,i} h^{enc}_i \tag{5}$$
$$u_t = [h^{enc}_i;\ a_t] \tag{6}$$
$$o_t = Dropout(Tanh(W_u\, u_t)) \tag{7}$$
$$y_t = Softmax(W_{vocab} o_t) \tag{8}$$

Where y is output token, h, c are hidden state and context, α is attention score, a is attention, o is combined output. $W_{attProj}$ and W_u are trainable parameters.

2. TOP dataset is available at http://fb.me/semanticparsingdialog

To better predict the word indexes in compact representation, we implement an attention-based copy mechanism, introduced by Eric and Manning (2017). First, we define the largest word index (utterance length) as system parameter and expand the decoder's vocabulary to include all word indexes from zero to the largest word index; then we modify the formula (6) to directly add the attention score α to compute the output tokens as below:

$$u_t = [h_i^{enc};\ a_t;\ \alpha_t]$$

Here, attention score is padded to the largest word index. The addition of attention score can provide useful signals to decoder to improve its prediction on word indexes.

We call the original model (without copy mechanism) as *vanilla seq-to-seq*, and the model with copy mechanism as *copy-augmented seq-to-seq*. In this paper, we make two hypotheses: 1. TOP parsers should benefit the shorten parses of compact representation and produce better inductive bias than LOTV representation despite the increase of token vocabulary size; 2. Copy mechanism should boost the prediction performance of seq-to-seq model.

Utterance: fastest route to the office today

LOTV: [IN:GET_DIRECTIONS 0 0 0 [SL:DESTINATION [IN:GET_LOCATION_WORK 0 0]] [SL:DATE_TIME_DEPARTURE 0]]

Compact: [IN:GET_DIRECTIONS [SL:DESTINATION [IN:GET_LOCATION_WORK]] [SL:DATE_TIME_DEPARTURE 5 6]]

Sig-wrd-idx Compact: [IN:GET_DIRECTIONS [SL:DESTINATION [IN:GET_LOCATION_WORK]] [SL:DATE_TIME_DEPARTURE 5]]

Sketch: [IN:GET_DIRECTIONS [SL:DESTINATION [IN:GET_LOCATION_WORK]] [SL:DATE_TIME_DEPARTURE]]

Fig 2: Examples of four representations in text format.

6 Evaluation

6.1 Representations

As mentioned before, with seq-to-seq model, LOTV representation can outperform base representation by large margin, so we exclude the base representation from the experiment. Besides LOTV and compact representations, we introduce two additional representations: *single-word-index compact representation* and *sketch*. In compact representation, a slot's content is denoted as a pair of word indexes, and it can be further reduced to a single word index for those slots that have exactly one word in its content. We would like to find out if this further token-size decrease by single-word-index compact representation can produce more inferencing benefits than compact representation.

As LOTV, compact and single-word-index compact representations share the same tree skeleton (nonterminal nodes) and only differ in leaves (terminal nodes), we extract the tree skeleton as a standalone representation, called *sketch*. We think studying sketch representation can help better understanding the nonterminal and terminal's contributions to prediction overheads among peer representations. Note that translating to a sketch parse cannot accomplish a TOP task by itself, as the parse has no slot contents (web API parameters). The sketch idea is inspired by Dong and Lapata (2018). Figure 2 shows an example of four representations in the experiment. Statistics of token lengths and vocabulary sizes of the representations are presented in Table 1.

Reps	*Non-terminal Len*	*Terminal Len*	*Total Len*	*Vocab Size*
LOTV	8	9	17	60
Compact	8	4	12	93
Sig-wrd-idx Compact	8	3	11	93
Sketch	8	0	8	59

Table 1: Average token lengths of four representations in test dataset (right bracket is counted as nonterminal)

6.2 Configurations

We use vanilla seq-to-seq model with LOTV representation as baseline and compare it with four other configurations: vanilla seq-to-seq model with compact representation; copy-augmented seq-to-seq model with compact representation; copy-augmented seq-to-seq model with single-word-index compact representation; and vanilla seq-to-seq with sketch representation. We choose exact match accuracy as metrics in this work, which is percentage of full trees that are correctly predicted.

6.3 Hyperparameters

Similar to previous TOP work, we use pre-trained 200b GloVe embeddings (Pennington at el. 2014). To make comparison fair, we ensure all four configurations share almost same set of hyper parameters: fixed random seed, batch size is 32; source input embedding size is 200; target input embedding size is 128; both encoder and decoder hidden size are 512; drop out value is 0.5; using Adam optimizer (Kingma and Ba, 2014) with learning rate 0.001 and decay rate 0.5; using cross entropy as loss function; running 50 epochs with early stops; top 2 beam search in inference.

6.4 Results

The main results are shown in Table 2. It can be observed that configuration 2 clearly outperforms configuration 1 by 2.61%, which confirms the first hypotheses: shorter token sequences are easier to learn and inference than longer token sequences, even with bigger-size vocabulary. One explanation is that compact representation has small vocabulary size (94), and seq-to-seq model is complex and powerful enough to accommodate the small increase of vocabulary size such that the performance of token prediction doesn't drop much. On the other hand, the longer token sequence makes the probability of exact match get worse quickly due to compounding conditional probabilities in a series of token predictions

Config ID	Model	Reps	Acc	Time (Sec)
1	Vanilla Seq2seq	LOTV	78.41	35
2	Vanilla Seq2seq	Compact	81.02	34
3	Copy-augmented Seq2seq	Compact	**81.68**	35
4	Copy-augmented Seq2seq	Sig-wrd-idx Compact	81.06	33
5	Vanilla Seq2seq	Sketch	84.03	28
6	RNNG Parser	Base	80.63	-
7	Span-based Parser	Base	**81.80**	-

Table 2. Exact match accuracies and training time per epoch of five configurations and two constituency parsers.

The configuration 3 performs better than the configuration 2 with edge of 0.66%, which confirms the second hypotheses: copy mechanism helps improving the word index prediction. Originally, learning word indexes requires model to have certain reasoning capability: connecting a 'word index' token to actual position in source utterance. In general, neural network is good at pattern recognition and but weak in reasoning. Copy mechanism can reduce the reasoning barrier and allows more leverage of neural network's strength in pattern recognition.

Comparing with compact representation, single-word-index compact representation has shorter token length, but its prediction performance gets worse, as observed in configuration 4's result. One possible reason is that compact representation has more predictable (word index) token occurrence pattern: its word index tokens always show up in pair right after a slot token, while single-word-index compact representation may have one or two word index tokens after a slot token, making tokens more unpredictable.

The configuration 5's result reveals the upper bound of other four configurations. The gap between configuration 3 and 5 is relatively small (2.35%), so we think the future research should pay more attention to improving the sketch's prediction, which is 84.03% at the point. Last, it can be seen that configuration 2, 3 and 4's accuracy results are comparable to two constituency parsers (Shah et al., 2018; Pasupat et al., 2019).

Config ID	Nonterminal Errors	Terminal Errors	Total Errors
1	1553	1188	1779
2	1300	971	1564
3	1243	945	1510
4	1293	987	1561
5	1316	0	1316

Table 3. Error counts of five configurations.

Error analysis. We count three types of inference errors in test dataset: nonterminal sequence (sketch) match errors; terminal sequence match errors; all token sequence match errors. When computing terminal sequence errors, consecutive terminals in a span are concatenated and treated as a single token. The result is listed in Table 3. Other than re-confirming the observations and arguments mentioned above, we have two new findings: 1. the copy mechanism seems able to boost both terminal and nonterminal inferences at same time (based on configuration 2 and 3's results). This is probably caused by the fact that decoder also gets some helpful clues from attention scores when predicting nonterminal tokens; 2. Compact representation (configuration 2 and 3) have less nonterminal errors than sketch representation (configuration 5). One possible explanation is that terminal (word index) token adds more contexts when predicting nonterminal tokens, e.g., if previous token is a word index, then current token cannot be intent, which narrows down the scope of token prediction.

7 Conclusions

In this paper, we propose a compact representation for TOP, which is more friendly to seq-to-seq parsers and demonstrates better performance than base representation and LOTV representation. It opens up another door to improve the semantic parsing for task oriented dialog.

References

D. G. Bobrow, R. M. Kaplan, M. Kay, D. A. Norman, H. S. Thompson, and T. Winograd. 1977. *GUS, A Frame-Driven Dialog System*. Artificial Intelligence, 8:155–173.

M. Eric and C. D. Manning. 2017. *A copy-augmented sequence-to-sequence architecture gives good performance on task-oriented dialogue*. SIGDIAL .

L. Dong and M. Lapata. 2016. *Language to logi- cal form with neural attention.* In Proceedings of the 54th Annual Meeting of the Association for Computational Linguistics, pages 33–43, Berlin, Germany.

L. Dong and M. Lapata. *Coarse-to-fine decoding for neural semantic parsing.* 2018. arXiv preprint arXiv:1805.04793.

C. Dyer, A. Kuncoro, M. Ballesteros, and N. A. Smith. 2016. *Recurrent neural network grammars*. In Proc. of NAACL.

A. Einolghozati, P. Pasupat, S. Gupta, R. Shah, M. Mohit, M. Lewis, and L. Zettlemoyer. 2018. *Improving semantic parsing for task oriented dialog*. In Conversational AI Workshop at NeurIPS.

D. Gaddy, Mitchell Stern, and Dan Klein. 2018. *What's going on in neural constituency parsers? an analysis.* In North American Association for Computational Linguistics: Human Language Technologies (NAACL-HLT).

A. K. Goyal, A. Metallinou, and S. Matsoukas. *Fast and Scalable Expansion of Natural Language Understanding Functionality for Intelligent Agents.* 2018. In Proceedings of the 2018 Conference of the North American Chapter of the Association for Computational Linguistics: Human Language Technologies, Volume 3 (Industry Papers). Association for Computational Linguistics.

S. Gupta, R. Shah, M. Mohit, A. Kumar, and M. Lewis. 2018. *Semantic parsing for task oriented dialog using hierarchical representations*. In Proceedings of the 2018 Conference on Empirical Methods in Natural Language Processing (EMNLP).

Sepp Hochreiter and Jürgen Schmidhuber. 1997. *Long short-term memory.* Neural computation, 9(8):1735–1780.

R. Jia and P. Liang. 2016. *Data recombination for neural semantic parsing*. In Proceedings of the 54th Annual Meeting of the Association for Computational Linguistics, pages 12–22, Berlin, Germany.

D. Jurafsky, and J. H. Martin. 2019. *Speech and language processing: An introduction to natural language processing computational linguistics and speech recognition,* (Version 3).

D. P. Kingma and J. Ba. 2014. *Adam: A method for stochastic optimization*. arXiv preprint arXiv:1412.6980.

B. Liu and I. Lane. 2016. *Attention-based recur- rent neural network models for joint intent detection and slot filling*. In INTERSPEECH.

P. Pasupat, S. Gupta, R. Shah, M. Lewis, and L. Zettlemoyer. 2019. *Span-based Hierarchical Semantic Parsing for Task-Oriented Dialog*. In Proceedings of the 2019 Conference on Empirical Methods in Natural Language Processing (EMNLP).

J. Pennington, R. Socher, and C. Manning. 2014. *Glove: Global Vectors for Word Representation*. In Proceedings of the 2014 Conference on Empirical Methods in Natural Language Processing (EMNLP). Association for Computational Linguistics, 1532–1543.

Learning Adaptive Language Interfaces through Decomposition

Siddharth Karamcheti and **Dorsa Sadigh** and **Percy Liang**
Computer Science Department, Stanford University
{skaramcheti, pliang, dorsa}@cs.stanford.edu

Abstract

Our goal is to create an interactive natural language interface that efficiently and reliably learns from users to complete tasks in simulated robotics settings. We introduce a neural semantic parsing system that learns new high-level abstractions through *decomposition*: users interactively teach the system by breaking down high-level utterances describing novel behavior into low-level steps that it can understand. Unfortunately, existing methods either rely on grammars which parse sentences with limited flexibility, or neural sequence-to-sequence models that do not learn efficiently or reliably from individual examples. Our approach bridges this gap, demonstrating the flexibility of modern neural systems, as well as the one-shot reliable generalization of grammar-based methods. Our crowdsourced interactive experiments suggest that over time, users complete complex tasks more efficiently while using our system by leveraging what they just taught. At the same time, getting users to trust the system enough to be incentivized to teach high-level utterances is still an ongoing challenge. We end with a discussion of some of the obstacles we need to overcome to fully realize the potential of the interactive paradigm.

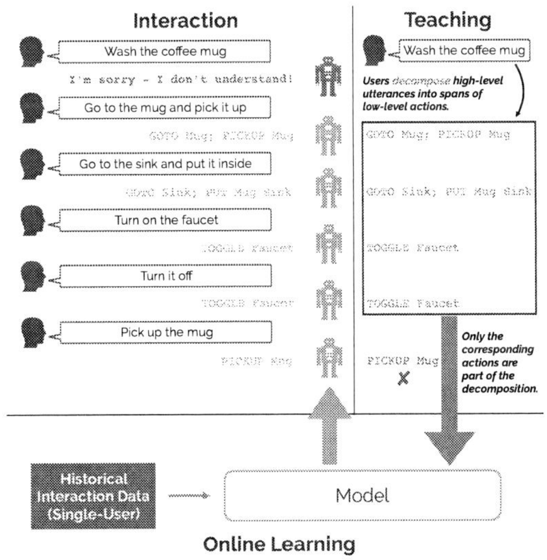

Figure 1: In our proposed framework, users interact with a simulated robot to complete tasks. Central to our approach is *learning by decomposition*: users teach the system to understand novel high-level utterances by breaking them down into utterances that the system can understand and execute. Using these decompositions, we update a semantic parser online, allowing our system to adapt to users as they complete more tasks.

1 Introduction

As robots are deployed in collaborative applications like healthcare and household assistance (Scassellati et al., 2012; Knepper et al., 2013), there is a growing need for reliable human-robot communication. One such communication modality that is both user-friendly and versatile is natural language; to this end, we focus on robust natural language interfaces (NLIs) that can map utterances to executable behavior (Tellex et al., 2011; Artzi and Zettlemoyer, 2013; Thomason et al., 2015; Arumugam et al., 2017; Shridhar et al., 2020).

Most existing work on NLIs (and AI systems more broadly) falls into a static train-then-deploy paradigm: models are first trained on large datasets of (language, action) pairs and then deployed, with the hope they will reliably generalize to new utterances. Yet, what happens when such models make mistakes or are faced with types of utterances unseen at training — for example, providing a household robot with a novel utterance like "wash the coffee mug?" Such static systems will fail with no way to recover, burdening the user to find alternate utterances to accomplish the task (or give up). Instead, we argue that NLIs need to be dynamic and adaptive, learning interactively from user feedback

Proceedings of the First Workshop on Interactive and Executable Semantic Parsing, pages 23–33
Online, November 19, 2020. ©2020 Association for Computational Linguistics
https://doi.org/10.18653/v1/P17

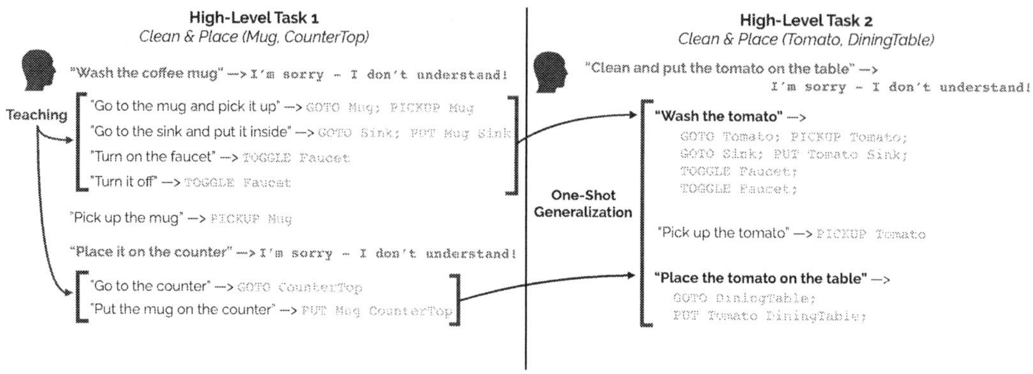

Figure 2: One-shot generalization example: When the system fails to understand an utterance (e.g. "wash the coffee mug", "place it on the counter"), the user teaches the system by *decomposing* it into other utterances the system can understand (illustrated by brackets above), which eventually get mapped to low-level actions that are executed. This induced mapping of high-level utterance to low-level actions forms an example that we use to update our semantic parser online. Because our semantic parser is capable of reliable *one-shot generalization*, users can leverage these decompositions when completing the next task.

to index and perform more complicated behaviors.

In this work, we explore building NLIs for simulated robotics that learn from real humans. Inspired by Wang et al. (2017), we leverage the idea of *learning from decomposition* to learn new abstractions. Just like how a human interactively teaches a new task to a friend by breaking it down, users interactively teach our system by simplifying utterances that the system cannot understand (e.g. "wash the coffee mug") into lower-level utterances that it can (e.g. "go to the coffee mug and pick it up", "go to the sink and put it inside", etc. — see Figure 1).

To map language to executable behavior, Wang et al. (2017) and Thomason et al. (2019) built adaptive NLIs that leverage grammar-based parsers that allow reliable *one-shot generalization* but lack *lexical flexibility*. For example, a grammar-based system that understands how to "wash the coffee mug" may not generalize to "clean the mug." Meanwhile, recent semantic parsers are based primarily on neural sequence-to-sequence models (Dong and Lapata, 2016; Jia and Liang, 2016; Guu et al., 2017). While these models excel from a *lexical flexibility* perspective, they lack the ability to perform reliable *one-shot generalization*: it is difficult to train them to generalize from individual examples (Koehn and Knowles, 2017).

In this paper we propose a new interactive NLI that is *lexically flexible* and can *reliably and efficiently perform one-shot generalization*. We introduce a novel exemplar-based neural network semantic parser that first abstracts away entities (e.g. "wash the coffee mug" → "wash the <obj>"), allowing for generalization to previously taught utterances with novel object combinations. Our parser then retrieves the corresponding "lifted" utterance and respective program (exemplar) from the training examples based on a learned metric (implemented as a neural network), giving us the lexical flexibility of sequence-to-sequence models.

We demonstrate the efficacy of our learning from decomposition framework through a set of human-in-the-loop experiments where crowdworkers use our NLI to solve a suite of simulated robotics tasks in household environments. Crucially, after completing a task, we update the semantic parser so that users can immediately reuse what they taught. We show that over time, users are able to complete complex tasks (requiring several steps) more efficiently with our exemplar-based method compared to a neural sequence-to-sequence baseline. However, for more straightforward tasks that can be completed in fewer steps, we see similar performance to the baseline. We end with an error analysis and discussion of user trust and incentives in the context of building interactive semantic parsing systems, paving the way for future work that better realizes the potential of the interactive paradigm.

2 Learning from Decomposition

User sessions are broken up into a sequence of *episodes* (individual tasks), each comprised of *two phases*: 1) *Interaction*, where the user provides utterances to the system to accomplish the task, and 2) *Teaching*, where the user teaches the system to understand novel utterances (Figures 1 and 2).

Primitive Action	Canonical Utterance
`GOTO <OBJ>`	go to <obj>
`PICKUP <OBJ>`	pick up <obj>
`OPEN <OBJ>`	open <obj>
`CLOSE <OBJ>`	close <obj>
`TOGGLE <OBJ>`	turn on/off <obj>
`PUT <OBJ> <OBJ>`	put object <obj>

Table 1: List of primitive programmatic actions and seed utterances used to initialize our semantic parser. Note that the utterances are *lifted*; they do not include references to concrete objects. This enables one-shot generalization to unseen object combinations.

2.1 Interaction

During interaction, the user attempts to complete a task by producing a sequence of user utterances $u_1, u_2, \ldots$ with the corresponding system responses $p_1, p_2, \ldots$ (including the `NOT-SURE` action) that are executed in the environment (the `NOT-SURE` action executes to an error message "I'm sorry - I don't understand!"). For example, in Figure 1, the user first says the novel utterance "wash the coffee mug," and the system returns `NOT-SURE`. The user follows up with "go to the mug and pick it up," which the system maps to the program `GOTO Mug; PICKUP Mug`. This continues until the user has completed the task. If the system or user makes a mistake and produces an undesired action, the user must continue to provide utterances, as there are no resets.

2.2 Teaching

The goal of teaching is to convert the sequence of utterance-action pairs (u_i, p_i) into a set of valid training examples for updating the system. To do this, the system presents the user with each u_i where p_i is `NOT-SURE`, and asks the user to select the corresponding contiguous sequence of actions $p_{i+1}, \ldots p_j$. To facilitate comprehension, we show users (programatically generated) human-readable representations of each action p — e.g. "go to the mug" for a program $p =$ `GOTO Mug`. For example, the user maps "wash the coffee mug" to the sequence `GOTO Mug; PICKUP Mug; ... TOGGLE Faucet` (see Figure 1 for the full decomposition). Similarly, the user maps "place it on the counter" to `GOTO CounterTop; PUT Mug CounterTop`. The resulting examples $(u_i, \hat{p}_i = p_{i+1} \ldots p_j)$ are used to update the system (details in Section 3.2.2). We update *every time* a user completes a task and teaches new examples — this allows users to access what they have taught immediately, during the following task.

2.3 Desiderata

This example illustrates two desiderata for our framework, both of which are key to *trust*: 1) the ability to identify novel types of utterances (when to output `NOT-SURE`), as well as 2) the ability to perform one-shot generalization. Knowing when to output `NOT-SURE` is key to *trust during inference*: signaling to users what the system knows, so that the simulated robot does not take undesired actions (like dropping your coffee mug on the floor). Performing one-shot generalization is key to *trust during learning*: users need to rely on the system remembering what has been taught so they can more efficiently complete future tasks. For example, when the user is completing the next task (second half of Figure 1), they should be able to rely on the system understanding "wash the tomato" and "place the tomato on the table," even though these refer to different objects than in the taught examples. Section 3 discusses how we enable one-shot generalization in further detail.

Sequence-to-sequence models fail. We found modern neural sequence-to-sequence models to be a poor fit in our setting. The biggest problem we found was their ability to handle novel utterances. Anecdotally, we found when given the novel utterance "wash the coffee mug," a neural sequence-to-sequence system trained on the seed set of utterances in Table 1 returned the program `OPEN Mug`, which does not even execute. These problems are exacerbated by the lack of training data; a single user's interaction only creates a handful of new examples, contraindicating the use of data-hungry sequence-to-sequence models (Koehn and Knowles, 2017).

3 Semantic Parsing

To address the above desiderata (identifying when to output `NOT-SURE`, and one-shot generalization), we incorporate two key insights into our approach. To identify when to output `NOT-SURE`, we look at the distances between a new utterance and the utterances in our training set, similar to the exemplar-based approach of Papernot and McDaniel (2018) — if an utterance is "close enough" to a training utterance, return the corresponding program, otherwise return `NOT-SURE`. To enable one-shot generalization, our parser operates over *lifted* versions of utterances and programs — versions that abstract out explicit references to objects (allowing for automatic generalization to new combinations of objects unseen during training).

We now describe our semantic parser, which maps a user utterance u and environment state s to the corresponding program p that best reflects the meaning of the user's utterance. In this work, a state s consists of a set of objects where each object is defined by a fixed set of features (e.g. *visibility*, *toggle status*, etc.). We define a program p as a sequence of primitive actions, where each action consists of a template (from Table 1) with arguments corresponding to object types. We conclude with a description of how we retrain our semantic parser using the newly taught examples from the teaching phase (Section 2.2).

3.1 Model

Our semantic parser (Figure 3) takes an utterance u and first abstracts out entities (Section 3.1.1), creating *object references* and *lifted utterances*. We parse these into *object types* (Section 3.1.1) and *lifted programs* (Section 3.1.2), which are combined (Section 3.1.3) and fed to a reranker that additionally uses the state s (Section 3.1.4) to identify the program p^* to execute.

3.1.1 Entity Abstraction & Resolution

We define an entity abstractor that maps an utterance u (e.g. "wash the coffee mug") to a lifted utterance f (e.g. "wash the <obj>") and a list of object references $\mathcal{O}$ (e.g. ["coffee mug"]). The entity resolver maps each object reference $o \in \mathcal{O}$ (e.g. "coffee mug") to a grounded object type g (e.g. `Mug`) resulting in a new list $\mathcal{G}$. To do this, we exploit a set of "typical names," (e.g. `Mug` = {"coffee mug", "mug", "cup"}) that we define a priori, looking up the object type with the given name. However, if there are multiple types that share the given name (e.g. in our dataset, table is a "typical name" for `DiningTable, CoffeeTable, SideTable`), we use the current state s to disambiguate: we fetch all the matching items in s and return the physically closest one.

3.1.2 Semantic Parsing

Central to our approach is the exemplar-based semantic parser that maps a lifted utterance f to a set of lifted programs $\mathcal{Q}$. To do this, we learn a classifier p_θ that takes two lifted utterances (f, f') and predicts a probability whether they have the same lifted program ($q = q'$). We take $\mathcal{Q}$ to be the programs corresponding to the highest probability f' under p_θ.

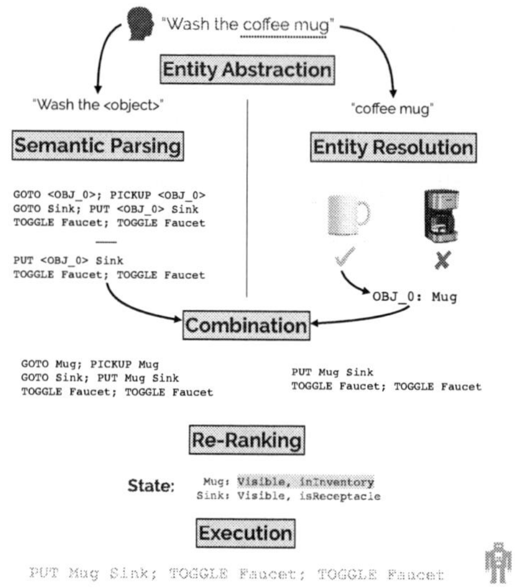

Figure 3: Semantic parsing pipeline. First, entities are extracted and the corresponding outputs — the lifted utterance and object references — are parsed into programs and grounded object types. These are combined and re-ranked to identify the program to execute.

Embedding Utterances. We first embed each utterance with an embedding function ϕ, implemented as a neural network that first uses GloVe (Pennington et al., 2014) to embed the words in f followed by position encoding similar to that used in Vaswani et al. (2017) and a nonlinear transform. The resulting embeddings are summed and fed into to a two-layer MLP to create the utterance embedding $\phi(f)$. The classifier p_θ outputs $\sigma(a \text{ cos-sim}(\phi(f), \phi(f')) + b)$, where cos-sim is cosine similarity, a, b are learned scalars, and σ is the sigmoid function. We train p_θ with a binary cross-entropy objective on a training set of (lifted utterance, lifted program) pairs: $\{(f_i, f_j, [q_i = q_j]) : i, j \in [n]\}$.

Efficient Inference. We now describe how we use p_θ for inference given a new lifted utterance f'. Unfortunately, naïve application of p_θ for a new f' requires pairwise comparison with *every training example*. We streamline this by using the structure of our embedding space — as the classifier outputs the scaled cosine similarity between two utterances, we store the embeddings $\phi(f_i)$ for each training utterance (f_i, q_i) in our dataset, then use an approximate nearest neighbors algorithm to find the the set of utterances that are "close-enough"; we use the corresponding lifted programs to form the output set $\mathcal{Q}$. We formalize what it means for an utterance to be "close-enough" in the following paragraph. We note that this procedure is similar to COSINEBERT (Mussman et al., 2020), a model used for active learning on pairwise language tasks.

Setting a Threshold. One of the desiderata of our system is returning `NOT-SURE` for utterances it is not confident about. To do this, we set a *threshold* τ such that if $\|\phi(f) - \phi(f')\|_2 \geq \tau$, return `NOT-SURE`. Note that this is equivalent to to thresholding the probability output by p_θ which is monotonic in the cosine distance as defined above. We set this threshold using a held-out validation set of (utterance, program) pairs (defined based solely on the seed examples in Table 1). For each utterance in the validation set f, we set τ such that 90% of the programs corresponding to utterances with τ are correct. Given an utterance f' at test time, we return the set of lifted programs $\mathcal{Q}$ corresponding to all lifted utterances within τ of $\phi(f')$ (all lifted utterances "close enough" to f').

Handling Compositionality. For multi-action utterances (e.g. "go to the apple **and** pick it up") we heuristically split on the keyword "and," resulting in multiple substrings. We parse each substring obtaining subsets of lifted programs, and take the cross-product of these subsets as the final set $\mathcal{Q}$. We acknowledge that this is not a perfect heuristic; in future work we hope to explore more general extensions that allow us to efficiently interpret utterances that have been composed in this way.

Implementation Details. When identifying the threshold τ, we define a hyperparameter lower bound β; this lower bound ensures that our semantic parser isn't overly conservative (returning `NOT-SURE` despite being moderately confident about the set of candidate programs). We find a value $\beta = 0.15$ works well for our experiments. We use Spotify's `annoy` library as our approximate nearest neighbors store for fast lookups.

We initialize our exemplar-based parser with seed examples (utterances mapped to programs) that cover the set of actions. Table 1 shows these actions, and a subset of the utterances used for training — our full dataset consists of only 44 examples (minor variations of the trigger words in the table). This is similar to prior work that defines a set of *canonical utterances* (Wang et al., 2015), or a *core grammar* (Wang et al., 2017). We strip stop words (*the, up, down, on, off, of, in, to, then, a, an, back, front, out, from, with, inside, outside, below, above, top*) from f prior to feeding to our parser to make our model more robust to minor lexical variation.

3.1.3 Combination

We combine each lifted program $q \in \mathcal{Q}$ with the grounded object types $\mathcal{G}$ to form a set of grounded programs $\mathcal{P} = \{p_1, \ldots, p_k\}$. In general, given a lifted program q that takes a sequence of arguments (e.g `PUT <OBJ> <OBJ>`) and a list of object types (e.g. $\mathcal{G}$ = [`Mug, DiningTable`]), we simply substitute the object types into the program, replacing each argument in the lifted program. This results in a final grounded program (e.g. p = `PUT Mug DiningTable`).

3.1.4 Reranking

The semantic parser, entity resolver, and combination step produce a set of grounded programs $\mathcal{P}$. The reranker takes the original utterance u, current state s, and this set of grounded programs $\mathcal{P}$ and chooses a single candidate $p^* \in \mathcal{P}$ to execute.

As a first step, we discard candidate programs that fail to execute in our simulator: for example, `PICKUP Mug` is discarded if the robot is already holding an object. Then we use a neural network to produce a score for each $p_i \in \mathcal{P}$. This network separately embeds the utterance, state, and each candidate program, feeding the concatenated embeddings to a two-layer MLP to produce a real-valued score for each p_i. In our work, the state s is retrieved dynamically based on the grounded objects $\mathcal{G}$ returned by the entity resolver; the state is made up of hand-coded features corresponding to attributes like *visibility*, *toggle status*, and *whether it can be picked up*, amongst others. We use a similar scheme as the semantic parser (Section 3.1.2) to encode utterances and candidate programs (embed, position encode, and sum), and a simple linear transformation to encode the bag-of-features representing the state s.

The highest-scoring candidate $p^* \in \mathcal{P}$ is executed. The reranker is trained via the process described in Section 3.2.3 *only after new examples are taught by users* during the teaching phase following each task they are asked to complete.

3.2 Retraining from User Feedback

In the following subsections, we discuss how to retrain our semantic parser and reranker to achieve the second of the two desiderata desired of our system: reliable and efficient *one-shot generalization*. As input to the retraining procedure, we take the dataset $\hat{\mathcal{D}} = (u_i, \hat{p}_i)$ of newly taught examples from the teaching phase (Section 2.2).

3.2.1 Creating Lifted Examples

Retraining the exemplar-based semantic parser requires converting our grounded dataset $\hat{\mathcal{D}}$ to pairs of lifted utterances and programs. Consider the grounded example ("Place the tomato on the table", `GOTO DiningTable; PUT Tomato DiningTable`); we want to map this to its lifted form ("Place the <obj> on the <obj>", `GOTO <OBJ> PUT <OBJ> <OBJ>`). To do this, we use the entity abstractor and resolver (from Section 3.1.1) to factor out object references.

Concretely, using the entity abstractor on the above example leaves us with $\hat{f}$ = "Place the <obj> on the <obj>", and references $\hat{\mathcal{O}}$ = ["tomato", "dining table"], which the entity resolver maps to $\hat{\mathcal{G}}$ = [`Tomato, DiningTable`]. We replace any element of $\mathcal{G}$ that occurs in the original program with the generic <OBJ> token to create the lifted program ($\hat{q}$ = `GOTO <OBJ>; PUT <OBJ>`). Applying this procedure to each example in $\hat{\mathcal{D}}$ gives us our lifted examples $(\hat{f}, \hat{q})$.

3.2.2 Updating the Semantic Parser

Updating the semantic parser requires optimizing the binary cross-entropy objective from Section 3.1.2 using these lifted examples $(\hat{f}, \hat{q})$. As we train our parser from pairs of examples, and there are far more negative examples (pairs with different programs) than positives, we over-sample positive examples so that batches have an equal number of positives and negatives. We train on the entire history of data for the given user, re-creating the nearest neighbors store with embeddings of each training utterance f_i. After this step, we recalibrate the nearest neighbors threshold using the procedure in Section 3.1.2.

3.2.3 Updating the Reranker

After updating the semantic parser, we re-parse each utterance in our dataset to define our retraining dataset of $(\hat{u}_i, \hat{\mathcal{P}}_i, \hat{s}_i)$ tuples. We use the program p^* that was actually executed for utterance $\hat{u}_i$ in state $\hat{s}_i$ as the "gold" label for the reranker. We train the reranker by maximizing the log-likelihood (minimizing the cross-entropy loss) of this candidate p^* amongst the others.

4 Experiments

We evaluate our approach with a set of human-in-the-loop experiments where crowdworkers are tasked with solving a series of simulated robotics tasks. Users interact with our system over 5 episodes (where each episode consists of a single task), teaching our system new examples after successfully completing each one. Each user has their own individual semantic parser and re-ranker (models are not shared across the users), with both components updating online after each teaching phase, prior to the start of the next task. Updating the two models (including rebuilding the nearest neighbors store) after each teaching phase varies depending on task complexity, but takes anywhere from 28 – 63 seconds on an Amazon EC2 T2.Medium (2 CPUs, 4 GiB RAM, no GPU) instance.

4.1 Experimental Setup

Environment and Tasks. Our experiments take place in simulated household environments, with users completing structured, everyday tasks. We create a 2D web-client inspired by the AI2-THOR Simulation Environment (Kolve et al., 2017) that removes the 3D rendering and spatial layout, but preserves the object types, attributes, and relations.

We borrow our tasks from the ALFRED Dataset (Shridhar et al., 2020) that defines 7 task types: 1) *Pick and Place*, 2) *Pick Two Objects and Place*, 3) *Look at Object in Light*, 4) *Nested Pick and Place*, 5) *Pick, Clean, and Place*, 6) *Pick, Heat, and Place*, and 7) *Pick, Cool, and Place*.

Interactive User Studies: We run our interactive user studies via Amazon Mechanical Turk (AMT). Each user is assigned one of the 7 task types, and is asked to complete 5 tasks of that type in a row. We recruited 20 workers per approach. Workers were paid \$5 with an average completion time of 23 minutes. We limit our AMT studies to workers with an approval rating $\geq 98\%$, location = US, and a total number of completed HITs > 5000.

Baseline. We compare our approach with a neural sequence-to-sequence with attention model similar to Jia and Liang (2016). To improve reliability, if the user enters an utterance that can be handled by a simple grammar that covers the core utterances

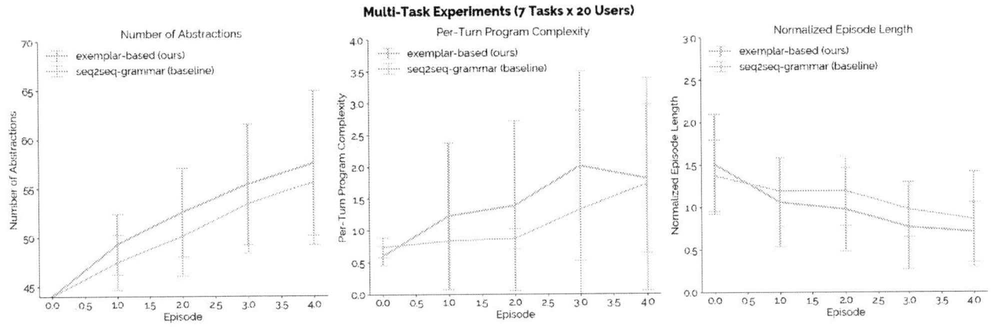

Figure 4: Complete set of results across 20 users with 7 different task types. Each user is given a single task type, and asked to complete 5 different episodes, with different combinations of environments and objects. The graph on the left shows the *number of examples taught* over 5 episodes. The graph in the middle shows the *per-turn program complexity* (number of primitives per language utterance) over time. The last graph shows the *normalized episode length* (# utterances to solve task / number of actions required).

from Table 1, we return the resulting program; otherwise, we invoke the sequence-to-sequence model. We find the inclusion of such a grammar necessary to prevent users from getting stuck. We refer to this combination of a neural sequence-to-sequence with a grammar as "*seq2seq-grammar*", whereas we refer to our system as "*exemplar-based*". We keep the learning by decomposition framework identical for both our system and the sequence-to-sequence system — in other words, we simply swap out our exemplar-based neural parser described in Section 3.1.2 for the *seq2seq-grammar* model.

Metrics. We define three evaluation metrics:

1. *Total number of examples taught*: The number of unique (utterance, program) pairs that the users teach the system across each teaching phase (as described in Section 2.2). This number starts at 44, the number of unique seed examples from Table 1. Higher is better — this metric indicates whether users are engaging with the system to teach high-level abstractions; a flat curve means that the users have finished teaching and are exploiting the examples they have previously taught.

2. *Per-turn program complexity*: the number of actions generated per utterance. For example, an utterance that generates the program `GOTO Mug; PICKUP Mug; GOTO Sink; PUT Mug Sink` has complexity of 4 — one for each primitive (`NOT-SURE` counts at 0). We expect a steep upward trend in this metric over time as users teach and reuse progressively more complex examples.

3. *Normalized episode length*: the number of language utterances the user provided divided by the number of primitive actions required to solve the task. This is the end-to-end metric we seek to optimize — values less than 1 indicate that users are able to tap into what they have taught to complete tasks in fewer steps.

4.2 Results

Full Results: 20 Users x 7 Tasks. Figure 4 presents graphs of the three metrics over the 5 episodes for each of the 20 users, split across the 7 different task. Error bars denote estimated standard deviation across all 20 users. Users of both our exemplar-based system and the sequence-to-sequence baseline teach a moderate number of new examples over time, with an upwards trend in per-turn program complexity as they complete more tasks. Finally, we see a decreasing trend in the normalized episode length, with the mean value of our system dipping slightly below a value of 1 after completing 5 instances.

Case Study: *Pick, Cool, and Place*. Figure 5, on the other hand, presents graphs of the 3 metrics across 3 users for the *Pick, Cool, and Place* task, one of the more complex tasks in our suite, requiring at least 12 primitive utterances to complete successfully (compared to tasks like *Pick and Place* that only require 4). Here we see large gaps between our system and the sequence-to-sequence baseline — not only do users of our system teach significantly more high-level examples, but they have a much-higher per-turn program complexity after 5 episodes compared to the baseline. Finally,

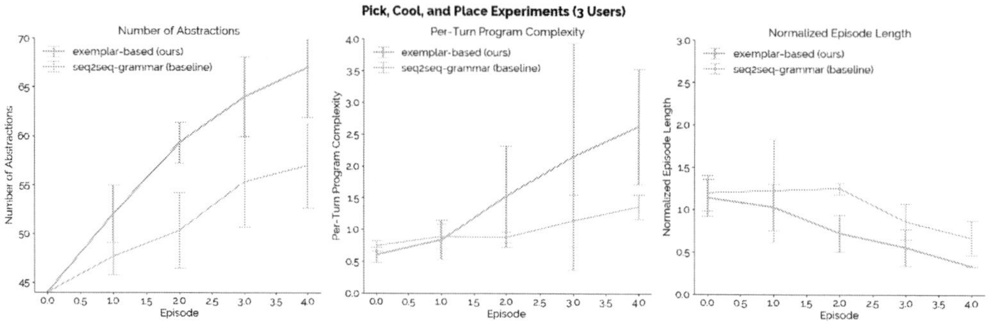

Figure 5: Results for the *Pick, Cool, and Place* task across 3 users (subset of the original 20). This task is complex, requiring at least 12 primitives to complete. Notice how the number of defined examples and per-turn program complexity are much higher for our method, and that the normalized episode length is lower.

we see that after 5 episodes, the normalized episode length is around 0.2, indicating that users are able to complete the complex task in 1/5 the steps necessary with our system.

Are users re-using high-level abstractions? The general results in Figure 4 indicate that while users are teaching the system new abstractions, they are unfortunately not re-using them effectively. The normalized episode length plot shows that both systems converge to 1, indicating that users are defaulting to the primitive actions, rather than trying to teach higher-level examples. One possible explanation for this is that for simpler tasks (e.g. *Pick and Place*), it is perhaps easier and faster to provide low-level utterances (those in Table 1), rather than teach new examples. Defaulting to low-level utterances also explains the lack of a significant gap between the sequence-to-sequence model and our model — in light of low-level utterances, the grammar does the heavy-lifting (in other words, we would not be invoking the sequence-to-sequence model at all). Indeed, across all 20 users for the *seq2seq-grammar* model, 89.9% of successfully parsed utterances (713 out of 793 total) were handled by the grammar, with only 10.1% handled by the seq2seq model (70 of 793 total).

However, this trend doesn't hold true for more complex tasks. Figure 5 shows that users are teaching and reusing a significant number of examples, completing tasks extremely efficiently. One hypothesis is to correlate task complexity with abstraction reuse (and thus, the ease by which users solve tasks), and while supported by the *Pick, Cool, and Place* results (Figure 5), we would require future experiments with a larger number of users before we can draw meaningful conclusions.

5 Related Work

We build on a long tradition of learning semantic parsers for mapping language to executable programs (Zelle and Mooney, 1996; Zettlemoyer and Collins, 2005, 2007; Liang et al., 2011), with a focus on using context and learning from interaction.

Contextual Semantic Parsing. In many settings, successfully parsing an utterance requires reasoning about both linguistic and environment context. Artzi and Zettlemoyer (2013) developed a model for parsing instructions in the SAIL Navigation dataset (MacMahon et al., 2006; Chen and Mooney, 2011) that leverages the environment context. Later, Long et al. (2016) introduced the SCONE Dataset, requiring building models that can reason over both types of context. More recently, Yu et al. (2019) introduced the large-scale Conversational Text-to-SQL (CoSQL) dataset that requires jointly reasoning over dialogue history and databases to parse user queries to SQL. We handle both linguistic context and environment context in our work, by decoupling semantic parsing from grounding; our lifted semantic parser handles linguistic context, while our entity resolver and reranker handle environment context.

Learning from Interaction. Closest to our work is Voxelurn (Wang et al., 2017), and its close predecessor SHRDLURN (Wang et al., 2016). Voxelurn defined an open-ended environment where the goal was to build arbitrary voxel structures using language instructions. We take inspiration from its teaching procedure where users decompose high-level utterances into low-level actions in the context of a grammar-based parser. Other work uses alternative modes of interaction to teach new behaviors. Srivastava et al. (2017) used natural language explanations to teach new concepts. Relatedly, Labutov et al. (2018) introduced LIA, a programmable personal assistant that learned from user-provided condition-action rules. Furthermore, Weigelt et al. (2020) introduce an approach for teaching systems new programmatic functions from language that explicitly reasons about whether utterances contain "teaching intents," a mechanism that is similar to our procedure for returning `NOT-SURE`. Once these "teaching intents" have been identified, they are parsed into corresponding code blocks that can then be executed. Other work leverages conversations to learn new concepts, generating queries for users to respond to (Artzi and Zettlemoyer, 2011; Thomason et al., 2019). Notably, Thomason et al. (2019) used this conversational structure in a robotics setting similar to ours, but focused on learning new percepts, rather than structural abstractions. Yao et al. (2019) defined a similar conversational system for Text-to-SQL models that decides when intervention is needed, and generates a clarification question accordingly.

General Instruction Following. Other work looks at instruction following for robotics tasks outside the semantic parsing paradigm, for example by mapping language directly to sequences of actions (Anderson et al., 2018; Fried et al., 2018; Shridhar et al., 2020), mapping language to representations of reward functions (Arumugam et al., 2017; Karamcheti et al., 2017), or learning language-conditioned policies via reinforcement learning (Hermann et al., 2017; Chaplot et al., 2018).

6 Discussion & Lessons Learned

Towards More Complex Settings. Our analysis in Section 4.2 suggests that situating our system in a more complex setting might allow us to truly see the benefits of learning by decomposition. One such setting is Voxelurn (Wang et al., 2017), with its open-ended tasks that allow for the definition of multiple different high-level abstractions with compositional richness. In contrast, the tasks in this work are linear, with similar sequences of primitives used to accomplish each high-level task.

Future work should use this insight and identify environments that are more complex and open-ended, where users are naturally incentivized to teach the system new abstractions that built atop each other, to facilitate performing more complex behaviors. In robotics, this might translate to building systems for cooking, perhaps taking inspiration from Epic Kitchens (Damen et al., 2018), where the set of high-level objectives (general recipes to follow, kitchen behaviors to imitate) is much larger, but where individual subtasks (low-level abstractions like slicing a vegetable, stirring a pot) are very common and generalizable. Other settings might include open-ended building tasks, either in the real world (Knepper et al., 2013; Lee et al., 2019), or in virtual worlds like Minecraft (Johnson et al., 2016; Gray et al., 2019).

On Trusting Interactive Learning. Users have an implicit expectation that after providing just a single example — say to "wash the coffee mug" — the system will know how to "wash the tomato" or even "clean the plate" immediately. However, existing machine learning is not built with such extreme data efficiency in mind; especially for harder types of generalization (e.g. to "clean the plate"), we cannot guarantee learning this in a single step. While in this work we show reliable one-shot generalization across objects in a simplified setting, the real-world is much more complex, and different entities merit different behaviors. For example, consider generalizing from "wash the spoon" to "wash the table"; a system like ours will try to execute the program taught in the first context (going to the sink, placing the object inside, etc.) to the second, leading to complete failure.

Part of the problem is a *lack of transparency*; after teaching an example, it is hard for a user to understand what the system knows. This impacts trust, and as a result, when the system makes a mistake interpreting a high-level utterance, users back off to using utterances they are confident the system will understand (mirroring our observed results). This suggests future work in building more reliable methods for one-shot generalization and interpretability, providing users with a clear picture of what the model has learned.

Acknowledgements

This work was supported by NSF Award Grant no. 2006388 and the Future of Life Institute. S.K. is supported by the Open Philanthropy Project AI Fellowship. We thank Robin Jia, Michael Xie, John Hewitt, and Chris Potts for helpful feedback during the initial stages of this work. We finally thank the anonymous reviewers for their helpful comments.

References

P. Anderson, Q. Wu, D. Teney, J. Bruce, M. Johnson, N. Sünderhauf, I. Reid, S. Gould, and A. van den Hengel. 2018. Vision-and-language navigation: Interpreting visually-grounded navigation instructions in real environments. In *Computer Vision and Pattern Recognition (CVPR)*.

Y. Artzi and L. Zettlemoyer. 2011. Bootstrapping semantic parsers from conversations. In *Empirical Methods in Natural Language Processing (EMNLP)*, pages 421–432.

Y. Artzi and L. Zettlemoyer. 2013. Weakly supervised learning of semantic parsers for mapping instructions to actions. *Transactions of the Association for Computational Linguistics (TACL)*, 1:49–62.

D. Arumugam, S. Karamcheti, N. Gopalan, L. L. S. Wong, and S. Tellex. 2017. Accurately and efficiently interpreting human-robot instructions of varying granularities. In *Robotics: Science and Systems (RSS)*.

D. S. Chaplot, K. M. Sathyendra, R. K. Pasumarthi, D. Rajagopal, and R. Salakhutdinov. 2018. Gated-attention architectures for task-oriented language grounding. In *Association for the Advancement of Artificial Intelligence (AAAI)*.

D. L. Chen and R. J. Mooney. 2011. Learning to interpret natural language navigation instructions from observations. In *Association for the Advancement of Artificial Intelligence (AAAI)*, pages 859–865.

D. Damen, H. Doughty, G. M. Farinella, S. Fidler, A. Furnari, E. Kazakos, D. Moltisanti, J. Munro, T. Perrett, W. Price, and M. Wray. 2018. Scaling egocentric vision: The EPIC-KITCHENS dataset. In *European Conference on Computer Vision (ECCV)*.

L. Dong and M. Lapata. 2016. Language to logical form with neural attention. In *Association for Computational Linguistics (ACL)*.

D. Fried, R. Hu, V. Cirik, A. Rohrbach, J. Andreas, L. Morency, T. Berg-Kirkpatrick, K. Saenko, D. Klein, and T. Darrell. 2018. Speaker-follower models for vision-and-language navigation. In *Advances in Neural Information Processing Systems (NeurIPS)*.

J. Gray, K. Srinet, Y. Jernite, H. Yu, Z. Chen, D. Guo, S. Goyal, C. L. Zitnick, and A. Szlam. 2019. Craftassist: A framework for dialogue-enabled interactive agents. *arXiv preprint arXiv:1907.08584*.

K. Guu, P. Pasupat, E. Z. Liu, and P. Liang. 2017. From language to programs: Bridging reinforcement learning and maximum marginal likelihood. In *Association for Computational Linguistics (ACL)*.

K. M. Hermann, F. Hill, S. Green, F. Wang, R. Faulkner, H. Soyer, D. Szepesvari, W. Czarnecki, M. Jaderberg, D. Teplyashin, M. Wainwright, C. Apps, D. Hassabis, and P. Blunsom. 2017. Grounded language learning in a simulated 3d world. *arXiv preprint arXiv:1706.06551*.

R. Jia and P. Liang. 2016. Data recombination for neural semantic parsing. In *Association for Computational Linguistics (ACL)*.

M. Johnson, K. Hofmann, T. Hutton, and D. Bignell. 2016. The malmo platform for artificial intelligence experimentation. In *International Joint Conference on Artificial Intelligence (IJCAI)*.

S. Karamcheti, E. C. Williams, D. Arumugam, M. Rhee, N. Gopalan, L. L. S. Wong, and S. Tellex. 2017. A tale of two draggns: A hybrid approach for interpreting action-oriented and goal-oriented instructions. In *First Workshop on Language Grounding for Robotics @ ACL*.

R. A. Knepper, T. Layton, J. Romanishin, and D. Rus. 2013. Ikeabot: An autonomous multi-robot coordinated furniture assembly system. In *International Conference on Robotics and Automation (ICRA)*, pages 855–862.

P. Koehn and R. Knowles. 2017. Six challenges for neural machine translation. In *NMT@ACL*.

E. Kolve, R. Mottaghi, D. Gordon, Y. Zhu, A. Gupta, and A. Farhadi. 2017. Ai2-thor: An interactive 3d environment for visual AI. *arXiv preprint arXiv:1712.05474*.

I. Labutov, S. Srivastava, and T. M. Mitchell. 2018. Lia: A natural language programmable personal assistant. In *Empirical Methods in Natural Language Processing (EMNLP)*.

Y. Lee, E. S. Hu, Z. Yang, A. Yin, and J. J. Lim. 2019. IKEA furniture assembly environment for long-horizon complex manipulation tasks. *arXiv preprint arXiv:1911.07246*.

P. Liang, M. I. Jordan, and D. Klein. 2011. Learning dependency-based compositional semantics. In *Association for Computational Linguistics (ACL)*, pages 590–599.

R. Long, P. Pasupat, and P. Liang. 2016. Simpler context-dependent logical forms via model projections. In *Association for Computational Linguistics (ACL)*.

M. MacMahon, B. Stankiewicz, and B. Kuipers. 2006. Walk the talk: Connecting language, knowledge, and action in route instructions. In *National Conference on Artificial Intelligence*.

S. Mussman, R. Jia, and P. Liang. 2020. On the importance of adaptive data collection for extremely imbalanced pairwise tasks. In *Findings of Empirical Methods in Natural Language Processing (Findings of EMNLP)*.

N. Papernot and P. McDaniel. 2018. Deep k-nearest neighbors: Towards confident, interpretable and robust deep learning. *arXiv preprint arXiv:1803.04765*.

J. Pennington, R. Socher, and C. D. Manning. 2014. GloVe: Global vectors for word representation. In *Empirical Methods in Natural Language Processing (EMNLP)*, pages 1532–1543.

B. Scassellati, H. Admoni, and M. Mataric. 2012. Robots for use in autism research. *Annual review of biomedical engineering*, 14:275–294.

M. Shridhar, J. Thomason, D. Gordon, Y. Bisk, W. Han, R. Mottaghi, L. Zettlemoyer, and D. Fox. 2020. Alfred: A benchmark for interpreting grounded instructions for everyday tasks. In *Computer Vision and Pattern Recognition (CVPR)*.

S. Srivastava, I. Labutov, and T. Mitchell. 2017. Joint concept learning and semantic parsing from natural language explanations. In *Empirical Methods in Natural Language Processing (EMNLP)*, pages 1528–1537.

S. Tellex, T. Kollar, S. Dickerson, M. R. Walter, A. G. Banerjee, S. J. Teller, and N. Roy. 2011. Understanding natural language commands for robotic navigation and mobile manipulation. In *Association for the Advancement of Artificial Intelligence (AAAI)*.

J. Thomason, A. Padmakumar, J. Sinapov, N. Walker, Y. Jiang, H. Yedidsion, J. W. Hart, P. Stone, and R. J. Mooney. 2019. Improving grounded natural language understanding through human-robot dialog. In *International Conference on Robotics and Automation (ICRA)*.

J. Thomason, S. Zhang, R. J. Mooney, and P. Stone. 2015. Learning to interpret natural language commands through human-robot dialog. In *International Joint Conference on Artificial Intelligence (IJCAI)*.

A. Vaswani, N. Shazeer, N. Parmar, J. Uszkoreit, L. Jones, A. N. Gomez, L. Kaiser, and I. Polosukhin. 2017. Attention is all you need. *arXiv preprint arXiv:1706.03762*.

S. I. Wang, S. Ginn, P. Liang, and C. D. Manning. 2017. Naturalizing a programming language via interactive learning. In *Association for Computational Linguistics (ACL)*.

S. I. Wang, P. Liang, and C. Manning. 2016. Learning language games through interaction. In *Association for Computational Linguistics (ACL)*.

Y. Wang, J. Berant, and P. Liang. 2015. Building a semantic parser overnight. In *Association for Computational Linguistics (ACL)*.

S. Weigelt, V. Steurer, T. Hey, and W. Tichy. 2020. Programming in natural language with fuse: Synthesizing methods from spoken utterances using deep natural language understanding. In *Association for Computational Linguistics (ACL)*.

Z. Yao, Y. Su, H. Sun, and W. Yih. 2019. Model-based interactive semantic parsing: A unified framework and a text-to-SQL case study. In *Empirical Methods in Natural Language Processing (EMNLP)*.

T. Yu, R. Zhang, H. Y. Er, S. Li, E. Xue, B. Pang, X. V. Lin, Y. C. Tan, T. Shi, Z. Li, Y. Jiang, M. Yasunaga, S. Shim, T. Chen, A. R. Fabbri, Z. Li, L. Chen, Y. Zhang, S. Dixit, V. Zhang, C. Xiong, R. Socher, W. S. Lasecki, and D. R. Radev. 2019. Cosql: A conversational text-to-SQL challenge towards cross-domain natural language interfaces to databases. In *Empirical Methods in Natural Language Processing (EMNLP)*.

M. Zelle and R. J. Mooney. 1996. Learning to parse database queries using inductive logic programming. In *Association for the Advancement of Artificial Intelligence (AAAI)*, pages 1050–1055.

L. S. Zettlemoyer and M. Collins. 2005. Learning to map sentences to logical form: Structured classification with probabilistic categorial grammars. In *Uncertainty in Artificial Intelligence (UAI)*, pages 658–666.

L. S. Zettlemoyer and M. Collins. 2007. Online learning of relaxed CCG grammars for parsing to logical form. In *Empirical Methods in Natural Language Processing and Computational Natural Language Learning (EMNLP/CoNLL)*, pages 678–687.

ColloQL: Robust Cross-Domain Text-to-SQL Over Search Queries

Karthik Radhakrishnan* Carnegie Mellon University kradhak2@cs.cmu.edu

Arvind Srikantan Salesforce Inc. asrikantan@salesforce.com

Xi Victoria Lin Salesforce Research xilin@salesforce.com

Abstract

Translating natural language utterances to executable queries is a helpful technique in making the vast amount of data stored in relational databases accessible to a wider range of non-tech-savvy end users. Prior work in this area has largely focused on textual input that is linguistically correct and semantically unambiguous. However, real-world user queries are often succinct, colloquial, and noisy, resembling the input of a search engine. In this work, we introduce data augmentation techniques and a sampling-based content-aware BERT model (ColloQL) to achieve robust text-to-SQL modeling over natural language search (NLS) questions. Due to the lack of evaluation data, we curate a new dataset of NLS questions and demonstrate the efficacy of our approach. ColloQL's superior performance extends to well-formed text, achieving 84.9% (logical) and 90.7% (execution) accuracy on the WikiSQL dataset, making it, to the best of our knowledge, the highest performing model that does not use execution guided decoding.

1 Introduction

Relational databases store a vast amount of the world's data and are typically accessed via structured query languages like SQL. A natural language interface to these databases (NLIDB) could significantly improve the accessibility of this data by allowing users to retrieve and utilize the information without any programming expertise. With the release of large-scale datasets (Zhong et al., 2017; Finegan-Dollak et al., 2018; Yu et al., 2018b), this task has gained a lot of attention and has been widely studied in recent years.

Prior research has primarily focused on translating grammatical, complete sentences to queries.

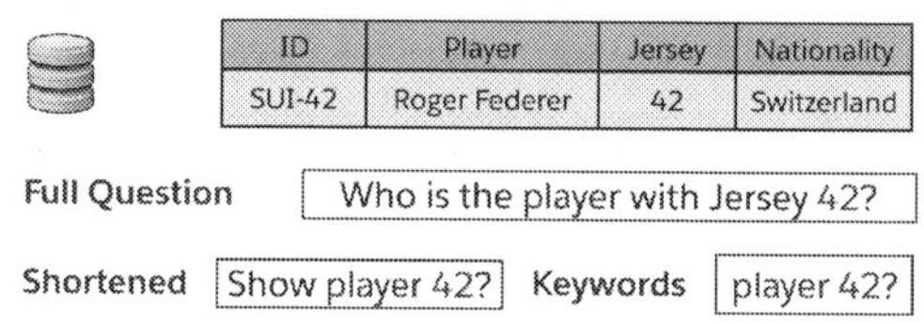

Figure 1: Examples of search-style user queries.

However, an internal user survey on the search service of a major customer relationship management (CRM) platform[1]revealed that users have a tendency to communicate in a colloquial form which could vary from using only keywords ("player 42") to very short phrases ("show player 42") to complete sentences ("Who is the player who wears Jersey 42?"). Apart from variation in style, users dropping content words from their searches in the interest of brevity also has the potential consequence of making their questions ambiguous. This could render the task unsolvable even to models accustomed to the NLS style of text. For example, in Figure 1, without the word "Jersey", it is impossible to identify which column's value (`Id` or `Jersey`) must equal 42.

In this work, we show that Text2SQL systems trained on only complete sentences struggle to adapt to the noisy keyword/short phrasal style of questions. To combat this, we introduce different data augmentation strategies inspired from our user search patterns and style. To tackle the induced ambiguity, a potential solution is to utilize the table content by allowing the model to scan the table for different terms present in the question and utilize that information to disambiguate (If the token "42" was only found in the `Jersey` column, then `Jersey` must be the column equal to 42). Though effective, this approach could become prohibitively expensive (in terms of inference time or memory

* This research was conducted during the author's internship at Salesforce.

[1]https://www.salesforce.com/

Proceedings of the First Workshop on Interactive and Executable Semantic Parsing, pages 34–45
Online, November 19, 2020. ©2020 Association for Computational Linguistics
https://doi.org/10.18653/v1/P17

required) on large tables as the model would have to search over the entire of the table content for every question.

We hypothesize that in most cases, the model only needs samples from the table content and not the exact rows that match tokens in the NLS question to disambiguate columns. For example, if the `Id` column contained alpha-numeric IDs, `Player` and `Nationality` contained strings, and `Jersey` contained two digit numbers, then `Jersey` must be the column equal to 42. Sampling alleviates the need of a full table scan for every question. The samples for each column could be generated offline and remain unchanged across questions or periodically refreshed (to reflect potential distribution shifts in the table or user queries), allowing for adaptation and personalization without retraining the model.

In summary, our contributions are as follows:

1. We augment the well-formed WikiSQL dataset with synthetic search-style questions to adapt to short, colloquial input.
2. We propose new models which incorporate table content in a BERT encoder via two sampling strategies to handle ambiguous questions.
3. We perform an in-depth qualitative and quantitative (accuracy, inference time, memory) analysis to show the efficacy of each content sampling strategy.
4. We curate a dataset of 400 questions to benchmark performance of Text-to-SQL models in this setting.

Apart from adapting to NLS style questions, COLLOQL also achieves state-of-the-art performance on the original WikiSQL (Zhong et al., 2017) dataset, outperforming all baselines that do not use execution guided decoding. We base our work off SQLova (Hwang et al., 2019) but our methods are generalizable to other approaches[2].

2 Related Work

Text-to-SQL approaches for the WikiSQL benchmark Text-to-SQL falls under a broader class of semantic parsing tasks and has been widely studied in the NLP and database communities. While early works have focused on pattern-matching and rule-based techniques (Androutsopoulos et al., 1995; Li and Jagadish, 2014; Setlur et al., 2016), with the introduction of large scale datasets such as WikiSQL (Zhong et al., 2017), recent works have focused on neural methods for generating SQL. They can be broadly categorized into a few themes - sequence to sequence (Seq2Seq), sequence to tree (Seq2Tree), and SQL-Sketch (logical form) methods.

Seq2Seq models frame the task as an encoder-decoder problem by trying to generate the SQL query token-by-token from the input question. However, as noted by Xu et al. (2018) these models suffer from the "order matters" issue where the model is forced to match the ordering of the where clauses. Zhong et al. (2017) employ reinforcement learning based method to overcome this issue but the gains from this has been limited as noted in Xu et al. (2018). Seq2Tree models generate the SQL query as an abstract syntax tree (AST) instead of a token sequence (Guo et al., 2019; Wang et al., 2020). These approaches define a generation grammar for SQL and learn to output the action sequence for constructing the AST (Yin and Neubig, 2018). Seq2Tree approaches are widely adopted for benchmarks that contain complex SQL queries (Yu et al., 2018b) as the syntactic constraints they adopt are effective at pruning the output search space and capturing structural dependencies. However, they do not show much advantage on the WikiSQL benchmark where the SQL ASTs are largely flat.

```
SELECT $AGG $COLUMN
WHERE $COLUMN $OP $VALUE
  (AND $COLUMN $OP $VALUE)*
```

Figure 2: SQL-Sketch from Xu et al. (2018).

SQLNet (Xu et al., 2018) introduces the concept of a SQL-Sketch, where it generates a sketch capturing the salient elements of the query as opposed to directly generating the query itself. SQLNet uses LSTMs to encode the question and headers and employs column attention to predict different components of the SQL-Sketch. As shown in Figure 2, the query is decomposed into different components which are predicted individually. TypeSQL (Yu et al., 2018a) extends upon this approach by augmenting each token in the question with its type (whether it resembles the name of the column, FreeBase entity type, etc). SQLova (Hwang et al., 2019) replaces the LSTMs encoder from SQLNet

[2]Our code and annotated data can be found at https://github.com/karthikradhakrishnan96/ColloQL.

and uses BERT to encode the question and headers jointly. Unlike SQLNet, SQLova does not share any parameters in the decoders and identifies the where clause values using span detection instead of pointer generators. HydraNet (Lyu et al., 2020) breaks down the problem into column-wise ranking and decoding and assembles the outputs from each column to create the SQL query.

Text-to-SQL with table content Recent works like NL2SQL-RULE (Guo and Gao, 2019), RAT-SQL (Wang et al., 2020) and Photon (Zeng et al., 2020) have looked into incorporating table content into the SQL generation. NL2SQL-RULE augments BERT representations with mark vectors for each question and table header token to indicate a match across the two parts. Photon only incorporates the content of a limited set of categorical fields when there is an exact match with a question token. Unlike NL2SQL-RULE, ColloQL includes table content in the BERT encoder allowing it to form content-enhanced question and header representations and unlike Photon, ColloQL incorporates content for all columns and includes samples even when there is not an exact match to disambiguate columns effectively. TaBERT (Yin et al., 2020) lifted the idea further by pre-training joint representation of text and table taking into account row subsampled in a random or relevance-based manner. The pre-trained joint representation has been shown to outperform vanilla language models in several table QA and semantic parsing tasks.

Text-to-SQL with execution guided decoding One common theme across all the high performing models on WikiSQL is that they all employ Execution Guided (EG) decoding. First introduced by Wang et al. (2018), EG is a technique where partial SQL queries are executed and their results are used to guide the decoding process. While EG has been shown to boost accuracy significantly, we do not apply execution guided decoding on our models for two reasons: Firstly, most EG methods modify the predicted query based on whether an empty set is returned. While this works well in the WikiSQL setting, having no results is often not due to an erroneous query. It is not uncommon for users to issue searches like "my escalated support cases"(with the expectation of surfacing zero records) or "John Doe leads"(to ensure that a record does not already exist before creating one) and we wanted to eliminate the reliance on database outputs to translate a query correctly. Secondly, database tables could have over 1M records and performing multiple database executions for every query could be expensive and is not always feasible whilst keeping up with the latency requirements of clients.

Text-to-SQL with noisy user input While recent text-to-SQL research typically focus on benchmark datasets with complete and grammatical input, noisy user queries are commonly encountered in practical NLIDBs. Previous work have proposed several ways to address this issue. Zettlemoyer and Collins (2007) introduced non-standard combinators to a combinatorial categorical grammar (GGG) based semantic parser to handle flexible word order and telegraphic language. Sajjad et al. (2012) and Yao et al. (2019a,b) developed interactive semantic parsing models that generate clarification questions for user to complete their underspecified queries. Arthur et al. (2015) paraphrases an ambiguous input into a less ambiguous form. Setlur et al. (2019) generates default logical forms for underspecified input. Zeng et al. (2020) synthesized a new dataset and trained question filter to identify noisy user input and prompt user to rephrase. Our work focus on handling short user utterances typically found in the search service of Salesforce CRM, where sampling-based content-aware models are effective at resolving most ambiguities.

3 Task and Datasets

The Text2SQL task is to generate a SQL query from a natural language question and the database schema/content. In this work, we use the WikiSQL dataset (Zhong et al., 2017) as it most closely matches the queries we expect to serve in a CRM. Our users typically don't issue linguistically complex queries requiring joins or nesting but instead focus on filtering a single table based on certain clauses.

WikiSQL contains over 80K natural language questions distributed across 24K tables and their gold SQL queries. The performance is typically evaluated on two different types of accuracies - Logical Form (LF) and Execution (EX). LF measures if the generated query exactly matches the gold query while EX executes the predicted and gold queries on the database and verifies if the answers returned by both are equal. Note that LF is a stricter metric as many different SQL queries could produce the same output.

NL Search	WikiSQL
acme opportunities	which opportunities are for acme account
John Doe accounts	where John Doe is owner what are accounts
deals with revenue >10	which deals have an expected revenue of over 10
number of deals closed in 2019	how many deals have closing year as 2019

Table 1: WikiSQL questions and their NLS-style counterparts.

The WikiSQL dataset mostly comprises of verbose questions which differ in style as compared to the NLS questions issued by our users. Table 1 shows NLS questions and their WikiSQL-style equivalents. To account for the differences in style, we augment the WikiSQL dataset with our synthetic data to simulate real-user NLS questions which is generated as follows.

Synthesizing user utterances from gold SQL labels Since WikiSQL contains the gold labels for the SQL sketch, we can use this data to generate NLS-style questions. By analyzing our user search queries (which resemble those shown in Table 1) we built question templates which we fill based on the gold SQL-Sketch. Some examples include shuffling the ordering of where conditions (users apply filters in different order), interchange ordering of column names and values (some users type "US region cases" while others type "region US cases"), and insert the select column name in the beginning or the end of a question ("John Doe accounts" vs "accounts John Doe"). The synthetic data is used in conjunction with clean well-formed queries from the original dataset, allowing the model to generalize to other queries not present in the templates. An example of synthetic utterances generated this way is shown below.

Original Query - Who is the player of Australian nationality that wears jersey number 42?

Generated Queries - *player jersey 42 australian nationality; 42 jersey australian nationality player; australian nationality jersey 42 player; ...*

Supporting relational symbols in user utterance We identify popular query ngrams when the conditional operator in the SQL-Sketch corresponds to either ">" or "<" and randomly replace these ngrams ("bigger than", "larger than", etc) with the operator symbols, allowing our model to properly interpret them.

Controlled question simplification Since WikiSQL contains no keyword-based questions and only a small portion of questions that are succinct enough to require reasoning over the table content, we employ a sentence simplification model followed by manual verification to create a test dataset to evaluate performance on NLS questions. A common user behavior is to drop unnecessary words from complete sentences to create shorter questions. We simulate this behavior by simplifying/compressing sentences to reduce verbosity. Note that keyword queries can be viewed as an extreme case of sentence simplification where only the required keywords are retained.

We make use of the controllable sentence simplifier by Handler and O'Connor (2019) to compress sentences to a desired length whilst retaining a specified set of keywords. We specify the list of keywords to be the header name of the select column, the values in the where columns (we ignore the header names for the where columns as users tend to omit them from their queries).

In total, we create two datasets: *short questions* with gold SQL labels and replacement of relation symbols, and *simple questions* with controlled sentence simplification.

Manually verified test set We create a high-quality test set by manually verifying a subset of *simple questions*[3]. A potential problem with sentence simplification models is ensuring that the shortened version still has enough information to execute the query correctly. This could vary based on the table content and is difficult to identify if the query is impossible to be executed correctly. We had a team of data scientists and engineers proficient in SQL to verify/correct outputs produced by the sentence simplification model and generated 400 queries for testing. We show examples in this dataset and report our manual quality evaluation in § A.1.

[3]Sentence simplification creates a diverse set of examples which contains some of those generated by gold SQL label.

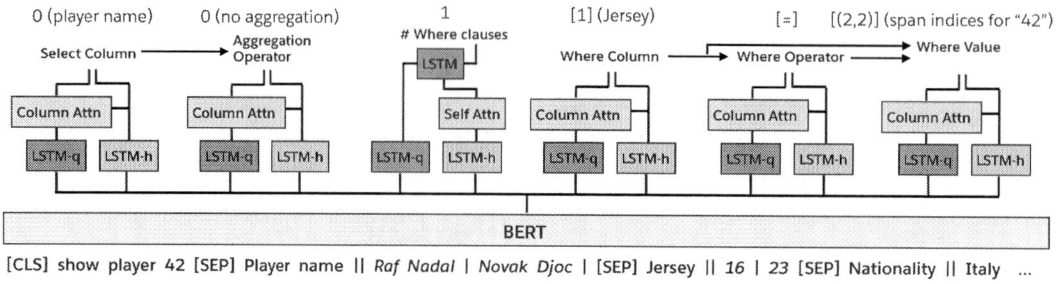

Figure 3: ColloQL uses the same NN architecture as SQLova where six decoding layers (one for each component of the SQL-Sketch) are used over BERT. The SQL query (`SELECT Player Name WHERE Jersey = 42`) is constructed from outputs of different components. Unlike SQLova, we also contextualize the question with the table samples (underlined in the figure) delimited by special tokens.

4 Proposed Approach

Following Xu et al. (2018) and Hwang et al. (2019), we decompose the SQL generation task into 6 different subtasks - one for each component of the SQL-Sketch. These subtasks all share a common encoder but use different decoder layers. The encoder is a BERT model (Devlin et al., 2018) which produces contextualized representations of the question, headers and the decoders largely use a task-specific LSTM with column-attention. Column-attention (Xu et al., 2018) is a mechanism where each header attends over all query tokens to produce a single representation over which a dense layer is used to predict probabilities.

The select, aggregation, where-num, and where-operator branches use LSTMs + Column-attention followed by a softmax layer to output probabilities. The where-column branch is similar but uses a sigmoid instead as multiple columns could appear in the where clause and the where-value outputs start-end spans for the values from the question.

Figure 3 highlights the architecture of our model. We retain the same encoder-decoder architecture as SQLova as our main contribution lies in the data augmentation and content sampling techniques to handle NLS questions.

4.1 Content Incorporation

As highlighted previously, table content could be a useful feature in helping the model disambiguate between different columns. Consider a table of tennis players as shown below.

Result	Court	Player
winner	clay	Rafael Nadal
runner-up	grass	Novak Djokovic
winner	hard	Jarkko Nieminen

Now, consider a question *"courts with Rafael Nadal as winner"*. A model which isn't informed about the content of the table cannot easily understand that Rafael Nadal needs to be the where clause value for `Player` and winner for the `Result` column. Allowing the model to scan the table for entities like "Rafael Nadal" or "winner" could help the model incorporate table content effectively.

Consider another question *"courts with Roger Federer as winner"*. It is intuitive that this query follows the same structure as the previous, except that the required value is now "Roger Federer". However, "Roger Federer" is not present in the table. We hypothesize that while table content is useful to the model, it does not need to be relevant to the query. The model, when given random samples of values for each column can infer the role of a particular column and generalize to unseen values which are similar to the column samples. In this work, we experiment with two sampling techniques - random and relevance sampling.

4.1.1 Random Sampling

Random sampling uses a fixed set of question agnostic column values sampled randomly (without replacement) and does not require access to the table once the samples are created. Since the sampling process can be done entirely offline, it adds negligible memory and time to the query execution. Additionally, the model can now be used in privacy sensitive scenarios as it does not access the table content and the samples could be manually configured. The model, now being content informed, performs better than its non-content counterparts whilst being more efficient than its full table content counterparts.

4.1.2 Relevance Sampling

Relevance sampling is used in cases where access to table is permitted and it includes a combination of samples relevant to question tokens and random samples. We index all cells of a table and perform a keyword search in the question to identify most relevant cells using FlashText (Singh, 2017) and include them as samples. In situations where the number of keyword matches are fewer than intended for a column or there are no matches, we fallback on random sampling to select the remaining samples.

To illustrate the importance of including random samples in the relevance sampling strategy, consider the following example:

Question - *Which countries hosted the MHL league?*
`League` **values** - NHL, MLB, NBA

Photon (Zeng et al., 2020), a model which only includes up to a single matched value, interprets this query incorrectly (`Select country where league = MHL league`). Its value matching approach retrieves an empty set to augment the table.[4] Our model with relevance sampling tackles cases like this successfully (`Select country where league = MHL`) as NHL, MLB, and NBA were included as samples because of the fallback on random sampling. Including random samples improves the model's ability to interpret questions that have values not directly found in the table.

The addition of random samples also allows the model to discriminate between columns effectively. Consider Question 4 from Table 2, the question is ambiguous without table content because it is unclear if the column to be selected is `Place` or `Country`. The pattern "where are... from?" indicates that the user's intent is to find a location and both column names seem like a reasonable choice (`Place` is a synonym for location and `Country` is a location). However, when augmented with random column samples, we see that the `Place` column only contains numeric values and is used as the synonym of "rank" in this table.

Figure 3 shows our input representation to the BERT model. Our representation bears similarity to Photon where the content values are concatenated along with the headers and the question separated by special tokens. However, Photon only tackles columns with picklists (categorical columns storing small fixed set of values) while we support numeric and free-form text columns as well. Additionally, as mentioned above, since Photon only incorporates a single matched value, it doesn't gracefully interpret all questions.

We concatenate the column samples to the headers with special delimiters and experiment with 1,3,5 samples for each column. The number of samples is currently limited by the maximum sequence length supported by BERT models and in the future we hope to experiment with operating on each column individually (Lyu et al., 2020) and diversity based sampling to extract the most distinctive samples.

5 Experiment Setup

We use the base version of BERT in all our experiments and made necessary changes for sampling on the original SQLova codebase. We use Adam (Kingma and Ba, 2019) optimizer with a learning rate of 1e-3 for the decoder layers and 1e-5 for the BERT model.

6 Results

6.1 Qualitative Examples

Table 2 shows some qualitative examples from our model when augmented with 3 values included for each column. The first two examples are based on random sampling and the latter two are based on relevance sampling. Our model is able to correctly resolve phrases such as "Maria Herrera" and "BMW" to the right columns when the corresponding values were not seen during training or inference. Consider the first two examples with different modifiers of "rider", leveraging the sampled values, our model correctly matches "BMW" to `Manufacturer` (column storing brand name like values) and "Maria Herrera" to `Rider` (column storing human name like values).

6.2 Effect of Random Sampling

We show performance of our model evaluated on the original WikiSQL dev dataset under different sampling settings. Owing to the 512 token limit, we only sample upto 5 values per column in Table 3. Modifying the architecture to operate on one column at a time (HydraNet) would allow us to use more samples. Our model performs significantly

[4] We ran the evaluation on Photon's demo page.

	grid of bmw rider with > 200 laps
	Rider || Nicolas Terol | Mike Di Meglio | Stevie Bonsey [SEP] Manufacturer || Derbi | Honda | KTM [SEP] Laps || 1 | 24 | 0 [SEP] Grid || 20 | 29 | 25 …
SQL	`SELECT (Grid) FROM 2-14125739-3 WHERE Manufacturer = bmw AND Laps > 200`
	grid of maria herrera rider with < 200 laps
	Rider || Nicolas Terol | Mike Di Meglio | Stevie Bonsey [SEP] Manufacturer || Derbi | Honda | KTM [SEP] Laps || 1 | 24 | 0 [SEP] Grid || 20 | 29 | 25 …
SQL	`SELECT (Grid) FROM 2-14125739-3 WHERE Rider = maria herrera AND Laps < 200`
	fox tv series female
	Animal Name || Jack | The Big Owl | The Wild Boar [SEP] Species || **Fox** | Badger | Boar [SEP] Books || No | Yes [SEP] Gender || male | **female** …
SQL	`SELECT (TV Series) FROM 2-11206371-5 WHERE Species = fox AND Gender = female`
	Where are Charlie Freedman/Eddie Fletcher from?
	Place || 7 | 9 | 1 [SEP] Rider || **Charlie Freedman/Eddie Fletcher** | Mick Horsepole/E … [SEP] Country || West Germany | Switzerland | United Kingdom [SEP] …
SQL	`SELECT (Country) FROM 2-10301911-6 WHERE Rider = charlie freedman/eddie fletcher`

Table 2: Some qualitative examples from our random (1,2) and relevance (3,4) sampling models. Bold values in headers indicate a match in the question.

better than our base SQLova model and performs competitively with other larger models.

Model	LF (dev)	EX (dev)
SQLova$_{\text{BASE}}$	79.5	85.3
SQLova$_{\text{LARGE}}$	81.6	87.2
HydraNet$_{\text{LARGE}}$ *	**83.6**	89.1
CᴏʟʟᴏQL $_{\text{rand:1}}$ †	82.0	87.6
CᴏʟʟᴏQL $_{\text{rand:3}}$ †	83.3	89.1
CᴏʟʟᴏQL $_{\text{rand:5}}$ †	83.5	**89.3**

Table 3: Model performance with different sampling settings. Rand:[1,3,5] uses random sampling. † indicates that data augmentation is added.

6.3 Effect of Relevance Sampling

In addition to random sampling, we also provide results on a model that finds the most relevant samples to the question. In Table 4, we compare our results with NL2SQL-RULE (Guo and Gao, 2019) (uses entire table content) and EM:1 (including a single exactly matched value), the content incorporation strategy adopted by Photon (Zeng et al., 2020). Since WikiSQL does not distinguish categorical columns, we applied the exact match to all columns. Our model achieves 85.2% logical form and 90.65% execution accuracy on the original WikiSQL dataset outperforming all models without EG.

Model	LF (dev)	EX (dev)
NL2SQL$_{\text{BASE}}$	84.3	90.3
CᴏʟʟᴏQL $_{\text{em:1}}$ †‡	82.5	88.2
CᴏʟʟᴏQL $_{\text{rand:3}}$ †	83.3	89.1
CᴏʟʟᴏQL $_{\text{rel:3}}$ †	**85.2**	**90.6**

Table 4: Efficacy of different content incorporation strategies. Relevance sampling (with 3 samples) gives the best performance. ‡denotes our implementation of Photon.

We also studied the memory and time footprint for indexing cells with increasing table sizes by benchmarking the performance of random and relevance sampling on very large tables. To simulate real-world data, we used IMDB movie database - a

* Due to unavailability of code, HydraNet numbers are only reported on datasets used in their paper

large-scale database with tables spanning over 7M rows containing movie metadata.

The random sampling method is agnostic to table size as samples are generated just once while the relevance sampling method scans the table to pick the best samples for each query. The results are shown in Table 5.

Model	Rows	Exec	RAM	Setup
COLLOQL $_{rand:3}$	1M	**0.2s**	-	-
COLLOQL $_{rel:3}$	1M	1.5s	4G	20s
NL2SQL$_{BASE}$	1M	200s	1.4G	-
COLLOQL $_{rand:3}$	7M	**0.2s**	-	-
COLLOQL $_{rel:3}$	7M	15s	18G	60s
NL2SQL$_{BASE}$	7M	x	8G	-

'-' → negligible; 'x' → practically intractable

Table 5: Benchmarking different content incorporation strategies with respect to execution time (CPU), memory footprint and setup time (for indexing).

6.4 Performance on Simple Questions

To measure the efficacy of content augmentation, we compared COLLOQL with other works on our dataset of 400 simplified queries which was generated by the sentence simplification model and verified/corrected by a team of data scientists and engineers. This dataset largely contains queries in which the where columns are not explicitly mentioned in the query and requires the model to infer them. We can see from Table 6 that a model uninformed of the content drops in accuracy (especially in the where column prediction) while COLLOQL retains its performance.

Model	LF	Where-col acc
SQLova$_{BASE}$	68.7	78.2
NL2SQL$_{BASE}$	80.8	94.3
COLLOQL $_{rand:5}$ †	83.2	92.2
COLLOQL $_{rel:3}$ †	**87.0**	**97.2**

Table 6: Performance on the curated test set i.e. 400 simplified queries.

6.5 Effect of Augmentation

Since SQLova was originally trained with complete sentences, it does not adapt well to short questions. Retraining the same model with augmented data from our templates recovers the performance (tested using short questions). Additionally, the augmentation also results in improved generalization resulting in a minor LF accuracy improvement on the original dev data as shown in Table 7.

Model	LF(short)	LF(dev)
SQLova$_{BASE}$	54.0	79.5
SQLova$_{BASE}$	86.2	80.6

Table 7: Comparing logical form accuracy of SQLova with augmentation. LF(short) is the dev accuracy on the short questions. LF(dev) is the accuracy on the WikiSQL dev split.

6.6 Performance on WikiSQL test set

Finally, we also show the performance of our model on the WikiSQL test dataset comparing them to the top approaches on the WikiSQL leaderboard[5]. As we can see in Table 8, COLLOQL achieves the highest accuracy without execution guided decoding on the WikiSQL test set.

Model	LF(test)	EX(test)
HydraNet$_{LARGE}$	83.8	89.2
NL2SQL$_{BASE}$	83.7	89.2
COLLOQL $_{rel:3}$ †	**84.9**	**90.7**

Table 8: Performance on the WikiSQL test set.

7 Error Analysis

We classified the errors made by our model on the ColloQL curated dataset into two major categories:

Aggregation - Given that WikiSQL contains noisy labels for aggregation component (Hwang et al., 2019) and the model was optimized for accuracy on WikiSQL, there are some errors in predicting this slot.

Select Columns - The simplified questions are often more ambiguous when predicting whether a column is a target to be selected or is used in a filtering condition (e.g. for the question "smallest tiesplayed 6 years", the model interprets it as `SELECT MIN(years) WHERE tiesplayed = 6` while the correct query is `SELECT MIN(tiesplayed) WHERE years = 6`). Additionally, we noticed that our annotators simplified column headers like "shortstop"

[5]https://github.com/salesforce/WikiSQL

and "rightfielder" to "SS" and "RF", making the question very difficult to solve.

8 Conclusion and Future Work

In this work we tackled the task of converting noisy (short, potentially ambiguous) search-like (NLS) questions to SQL queries. We introduced data augmentation strategies to adapt to the NLS style of text and a novel content enhancement to BERT via two sampling strategies - random and relevance sampling. Random sampling overcomes some of the performance / privacy challenges of incorporating table content and relevance sampling achieves state-of-the-art performance when access to table content is permitted. Finally, we also curated a new held-out dataset to evaluate performance against NLS questions.

In the future, we hope to explore different sampling techniques (based on user history, sampling to maximize discernment between columns) to enhance performance. Besides, our approach and dataset mainly target telegraphic queries that can be effectively disambiguated with table contents, which frequency occur in our search service. We plan to extend our work to handle other types of input ambiguities and other application domains.

Acknowledgments

We would like to thank Christian Posse and Mario Rodriguez for their support, help and invaluable feedback throughout the development of this work. We also would like to thank our team of expert annotators for their contribution.

References

Ion Androutsopoulos, Graeme D. Ritchie, and Peter Thanisch. 1995. Natural language interfaces to databases - an introduction. *CoRR*, cmp-lg/9503016.

Philip Arthur, Graham Neubig, Sakriani Sakti, Tomoki Toda, and Satoshi Nakamura. 2015. Semantic parsing of ambiguous input through paraphrasing and verification. *Transactions of the Association for Computational Linguistics*, 3:571–584.

Jacob Devlin, Ming-Wei Chang, Kenton Lee, and Kristina Toutanova. 2018. Bert: Pre-training of deep bidirectional transformers for language understanding. *arXiv preprint arXiv:1810.04805*.

Catherine Finegan-Dollak, Jonathan K. Kummerfeld, Li Zhang, Karthik Ramanathan, Sesh Sadasivam, Rui Zhang, and Dragomir R. Radev. 2018. Improving text-to-sql evaluation methodology. In *Proceedings of the 56th Annual Meeting of the Association for Computational Linguistics, ACL 2018, Melbourne, Australia, July 15-20, 2018, Volume 1: Long Papers*, pages 351–360. Association for Computational Linguistics.

Jiaqi Guo, Zecheng Zhan, Yan Gao, Yan Xiao, Jian-Guang Lou, Ting Liu, and Dongmei Zhang. 2019. Towards complex text-to-sql in cross-domain database with intermediate representation. In *Proceedings of the 57th Conference of the Association for Computational Linguistics, ACL 2019, Florence, Italy, July 28- August 2, 2019, Volume 1: Long Papers*, pages 4524–4535. Association for Computational Linguistics.

Tong Guo and Huilin Gao. 2019. Content enhanced bert-based text-to-sql generation. *arXiv preprint arXiv:1910.07179*.

Abram Handler and Brendan O'Connor. 2019. Query-focused sentence compression in linear time. In *Proceedings of the 2019 Conference on Empirical Methods in Natural Language Processing and the 9th International Joint Conference on Natural Language Processing (EMNLP-IJCNLP)*, pages 5969–5975, Hong Kong, China. Association for Computational Linguistics.

Wonseok Hwang, Jinyeung Yim, Seunghyun Park, and Minjoon Seo. 2019. A comprehensive exploration on wikisql with table-aware word contextualization. *ArXiv*, abs/1902.01069.

Diederik P Kingma and J Adam Ba. 2019. A method for stochastic optimization. arxiv 2014. *arXiv preprint arXiv:1412.6980*, 434.

Fei Li and Hosagrahar V Jagadish. 2014. Nalir: an interactive natural language interface for querying relational databases. In *Proceedings of the 2014 ACM SIGMOD international conference on Management of data*, pages 709–712.

Qin Lyu, Kaushik Chakrabarti, Shobhit Hathi, Souvik Kundu, Jianwen Zhang, and Zheng Chen. 2020. Hybrid ranking network for text-to-sql. Technical Report MSR-TR-2020-7, Microsoft Dynamics 365 AI.

Hassan Sajjad, Patrick Pantel, and Michael Gamon. 2012. Underspecified query refinement via natural language question generation. In *Proceedings of COLING 2012*, pages 2341–2356, Mumbai, India. The COLING 2012 Organizing Committee.

Vidya Setlur, Sarah E Battersby, Melanie Tory, Rich Gossweiler, and Angel X Chang. 2016. Eviza: A natural language interface for visual analysis. In *Proceedings of the 29th Annual Symposium on User Interface Software and Technology*, pages 365–377.

Vidya Setlur, Melanie Tory, and Alex Djalali. 2019. Inferencing underspecified natural language utterances in visual analysis. In *Proceedings of the 24th International Conference on Intelligent User Interfaces*, IUI '19, page 40–51, New York, NY, USA. Association for Computing Machinery.

V. Singh. 2017. Replace or Retrieve Keywords In Documents at Scale. *ArXiv e-prints*.

Bailin Wang, Richard Shin, Xiaodong Liu, Oleksandr Polozov, and Matthew Richardson. 2020. RAT-SQL: relation-aware schema encoding and linking for text-to-sql parsers. In *Proceedings of the 58th Annual Meeting of the Association for Computational Linguistics, ACL 2020, Online, July 5-10, 2020*, pages 7567–7578. Association for Computational Linguistics.

Chenglong Wang, Kedar Tatwawadi, Marc Brockschmidt, Po-Sen Huang, Yi Mao, Oleksandr Polozov, and Rishabh Singh. 2018. Robust text-to-sql generation with execution-guided decoding. *arXiv preprint arXiv:1807.03100*.

Xiaojun Xu, Chang Liu, and Dawn Song. 2018. Sqlnet: Generating structured queries from natural language without reinforcement learning.

Ziyu Yao, Xiujun Li, Jianfeng Gao, Brian M. Sadler, and Huan Sun. 2019a. Interactive semantic parsing for if-then recipes via hierarchical reinforcement learning. In *The Thirty-Third AAAI Conference on Artificial Intelligence, AAAI 2019, The Thirty-First Innovative Applications of Artificial Intelligence Conference, IAAI 2019, The Ninth AAAI Symposium on Educational Advances in Artificial Intelligence, EAAI 2019, Honolulu, Hawaii, USA, January 27 - February 1, 2019*, pages 2547–2554. AAAI Press.

Ziyu Yao, Yu Su, Huan Sun, and Wen-tau Yih. 2019b. Model-based interactive semantic parsing: A unified framework and A text-to-sql case study. In *Proceedings of the 2019 Conference on Empirical Methods in Natural Language Processing and the 9th International Joint Conference on Natural Language Processing, EMNLP-IJCNLP 2019, Hong Kong, China, November 3-7, 2019*, pages 5446–5457. Association for Computational Linguistics.

Pengcheng Yin and Graham Neubig. 2018. TRANX: A transition-based neural abstract syntax parser for semantic parsing and code generation. In *Proceedings of the 2018 Conference on Empirical Methods in Natural Language Processing, EMNLP 2018: System Demonstrations, Brussels, Belgium, October 31 - November 4, 2018*, pages 7–12. Association for Computational Linguistics.

Pengcheng Yin, Graham Neubig, Wen-tau Yih, and Sebastian Riedel. 2020. Tabert: Pretraining for joint understanding of textual and tabular data. In *Proceedings of the 58th Annual Meeting of the Association for Computational Linguistics, ACL 2020, Online, July 5-10, 2020*, pages 8413–8426. Association for Computational Linguistics.

Tao Yu, Zifan Li, Zilin Zhang, Rui Zhang, and Dragomir Radev. 2018a. Typesql: Knowledge-based type-aware neural text-to-sql generation. *arXiv preprint arXiv:1804.09769*.

Tao Yu, Rui Zhang, Kai Yang, Michihiro Yasunaga, Dongxu Wang, Zifan Li, James Ma, Irene Li, Qingning Yao, Shanelle Roman, Zilin Zhang, and Dragomir Radev. 2018b. Spider: A large-scale human-labeled dataset for complex and cross-domain semantic parsing and text-to-sql task. In *Proceedings of the 2018 Conference on Empirical Methods in Natural Language Processing*, Brussels, Belgium. Association for Computational Linguistics.

Jichuan Zeng, Xi Victoria Lin, Steven C.H. Hoi, Richard Socher, Caiming Xiong, Michael Lyu, and Irwin King. 2020. Photon: A robust cross-domain text-to-SQL system. In *Proceedings of the 58th Annual Meeting of the Association for Computational Linguistics: System Demonstrations*, pages 204–214, Online. Association for Computational Linguistics.

Luke Zettlemoyer and Michael Collins. 2007. Online learning of relaxed CCG grammars for parsing to logical form. In *Proceedings of the 2007 Joint Conference on Empirical Methods in Natural Language Processing and Computational Natural Language Learning (EMNLP-CoNLL)*, pages 678–687, Prague, Czech Republic. Association for Computational Linguistics.

Victor Zhong, Caiming Xiong, and Richard Socher. 2017. Seq2sql: Generating structured queries from natural language using reinforcement learning. *CoRR*, abs/1709.00103.

A Appendix

A.1 Test Set Quality

One of the authors who did not participate in the dataset annotation randomly sampled 16/400 examples and manually checked the quality. 4/16 annotations were found to have issues in the natural language annotation.

Table 9 shows examples from the *simple question* dataset. The first 4 examples are correct, high-quality annotations while the bottom 4 are those with issues found during manual check. The high-quality simple question annotations are readable and on average have a smaller compression ratio compared to the noisy annotations.

We noticed that some errors in the WikiSQL annotation (Hwang et al., 2019) were corrected when the simplified questions were produced, but some perpetuated through. In the second example, the annotator corrected spelling errors in the original WikiSQL annotation. However, in the 7th example, the original question misinterpreted `Year acquired` as a quantity and our simplified question inherited that error. Similarly, in the 8th example, the original question misinterpreted the field `Finalists` as "score" (it should represent "number of finalists") and our simplified question inherited it.

The 5th and 6th examples have unreadable questions as a result of sentence simplification (but our annotators still labeled them as correct). This is an artifact of the dataset as such unreadable, keyword-style queries may favor models that leverage table content to identify the columns. On the other hand, such queries could be useful as being able to interpret them may give users more flexibility when searching the content of a database.

Original	What is the amount of trees, that require replacement when the district is motovilikhinsky?
Simple	the amount of trees, that require replacement district motovilikhinsky?
	District || Total amount of trees || Prevailing types, % || Amount of old trees || Amount of trees, that require replacement || ...
SQL	`SELECT (Amount of trees, that require replacement) from _ WHERE District=Leninsky`
Original	How many winning drivers were the for the rnd equalling 5?
Simple	how many winning drivers for 5?
	Rnd || Race Name || Circuit || City/Location || Date || Pole position || Winning driver || ...
SQL	`SELECT COUNT(Winning driver) from _ WHERE Rnd=5`
Original	For the episode(s) aired in the U.S. on 4 april 2008, what were the names?
Simple	for the episode(s) aired in U.S. 4 april 2008, names?
	No. in season || No. in series || Title || Canadian airdate || US airdate || Production code ...
SQL	`SELECT (Title) from _ WHERE US airdate=4 April 2008`
Original	List the scores of all games when Miami were listed as the first Semi finalist?
Simple	scores with miami listed as first semi finalist?
	Year || Champion || Score || Runner-Up || Location || Semi-Finalist #1 || Semi-Finalist #2 ...
SQL	`SELECT (Score) from _ WHERE Semi-Finalist 1=Miami`
Original	What school did the forward whose number is 10 belong to?
Simple	what school did forward 10
	Player || No.(s) || Height in Ft. || Position || Years for Rockets || School/Club Team/Country ...
SQL	`SELECT (School/Club Team/Country) from _ WHERE No.(s)=10 AND Position=Forward`
Original	Which visitors have a leading scorer of roy : 25?
Simple	visitor of 25–18
	# || Date || Visitor || Score || Home || Leading scorer || Attendance || Record || Streak ...
SQL	`SELECT (Visitor) from _ WHERE Leading scorer=Roy : 25`
Original	how any were gained as the chan
Simple	how many gained chan
	City || Station || Year acquired || Primary programming source || Other programming sources ...
SQL	`SELECT COUNT(Year acquired) from _ WHERE Station=CHAN`
Original	What are the names that had a finalist score of 2??
Simple	names that had finalist score 2?
	School || Winners || Finalists || Total Finals || Year of last win
SQL	`SELECT (School) from _ WHERE Finalists=2`

Table 9: Examples in *simple questions* dev set. We use "_" as placeholder for table in the SQL queries. Only table headers were shown. The top 4 examples are correct while the bottom 4 have issue in the natural language annotation.

Natural Language Response Generation from SQL with Generalization and Back-translation

Saptarashmi Bandyopadhyay
University of Maryland, College Park
College Park, MD 20742
sapta.band59@gmail.com

Tianyang Zhao
The Pennsylvania State University
University Park, PA 16802
zty12713@gmail.com

Abstract

Generation of natural language responses to the queries of structured language like SQL is very challenging as it requires generalization to new domains and the ability to answer ambiguous queries among other issues. We have participated in the CoSQL shared task organized in the IntEx-SemPar workshop at EMNLP 2020. We have trained a number of Neural Machine Translation (NMT) models to efficiently generate the natural language responses from SQL. Our shuffled back-translation model has led to a BLEU score of 7.47 on the unknown test dataset. In this paper, we will discuss our methodologies to approach the problem and future directions to improve the quality of the generated natural language responses.

1 Introduction

Natural language interfaces to databases (NLIDB) has been the focus of many research works, including a shared track on the Conversational text-to-SQL Challenge at EMNLP-IntexSemPar 2020 (Yu et al., 2019). We have focused on the second task, natural language response generation from SQL queries and execution results.

For example, when the SQL query "SELECT dorm_name FROM dorm" is present, a possible response by the system could be "This is the list of the names of all the dorms". The ideal responses should demonstrate the results of the query, present the logical relationship between the query objects and the results, and be free from any grammatical error. Another challenge for this task is that the system needs to be able to generalize and do well on the SQL queries and the database schema which it has never seen before.

2 Related Works

Many existing papers focus on text to SQL generation like Shin (2019) and Zhong et al. (2017) which emphasize self-attention and reinforcement-learning-based approaches. The problem of generating natural language responses from SQL is that this specific area is relatively under-researched, but we have tried to come up with probable solutions in this shared task.

Gray et al. (1997) inspired us to generalize SQL keywords for better response generation with improvement in generalization. We have employed back-translation, used by Sennrich et al. (2015) and Hoang et al. (2018), in order to increase the BLEU score. We were also motivated by the linguistic generalization results pointed out by Bandyopadhyay (2019) and Bandyopadhyay (2020) where the lemma and the Part-of-Speech tag are added to the natural language dataset for better generalization. Although we did not include it in our final model due to challenges in removing the linguistic factors, this approach offers a potential future in the generalization of the generated natural language responses.

3 Pre-processing Methods

We decided to take the Neural Machine Translation (NMT) approach, where the SQL queries with the execution results are regarded as the source, and the natural language, more specifically English, responses are seen as the target. We chose Seq2seq as our baseline model. After several attempts of training and parameter tuning, we were able to obtain a baseline BLEU score.

In order to further improve the BLEU score, first, we came up with the idea of SQL keyword generalization. SQL keyword generalization is a pre-processing method we applied to the input data (i.e. the SQL queries with the execution results). We

Proceedings of the First Workshop on Interactive and Executable Semantic Parsing, pages 46–49
Online, November 19, 2020. ©2020 Association for Computational Linguistics
https://doi.org/10.18653/v1/P17

Original Keywords	Generalization
UNION, INTERSECTION, EXCEPT	SET
AND, OR	LOGIC
EXISTS, UNIQUE, IN	NEST
ANY, ALL	RANGE
AVG, COUNT, SUM, MAX, MIN	AGG

Table 1: The grouped SQL keywords and their substitutions.

first put the common SQL keywords into different groups based on their characteristics. Table 1 shows our choices of grouping. Then, we substituted each of those keywords in the input data to the newly purposed, generalized name according to the group we put the keyword in.

More specifically, UNION, INTERSECTION, and EXCEPT are substituted as SET because these three keywords are set operations. AND and OR are substituted as LOGIC because they are logic operators. One thing worth noting is that although AND in SQL is not only a logic operator as it can also be used to join tables, the phrase "JOIN ... ON ..." is primarily used for this particular purpose. EXISTS, UNIQUE, and IN are substituted as NEST because these keywords are followed by one or multiple nested queries. ANY and ALL are substituted as RANGE since they are followed by a sub-query that will return a range of values, and an operator such as $>$ is usually in front of ANY and ALL to compare with those values returned by the sub-query. AVG, COUNT, SUM, MAX, and MIN are substituted as AGG since all these keywords are aggregate operators.

The remaining common SQL keywords are difficult to be grouped with other ones. For example, GROUP BY and HAVING have distinct meanings and work differently as they are followed by non-identical elements. GROUP BY is followed by a "grouping-list", usually an attribute of a table, while HAVING is followed by a "group-qualification", usually a comparison involving an operator. Therefore, those keywords are kept as they are in the input data. Moreover, the operators are also not generalized since $>$, $\geq$, $<$, $\leq$ are used to compare numerical values only, while $=$ and $\neq$ are used to compare non-numerical values as well, like strings.

Overall, the reason we applied this SQL keyword generalization pre-processing is to avoid situations where certain common keywords are seen only for a few times or even never seen in the training data set, then the trained model would react poorly to those keywords in the test data set by pulling words from the vocabulary almost randomly.

4 Shuffled Back-Translation

Another idea we utilized to improve the BLEU score is the iterative back-translation as described in Shin (2019) and Zhong et al. (2017).

Back-translation is a simple way of adding synthetic data to the training model by training a target-to-source model, then generating a synthetic source dataset using a monolingual corpus on the target side. The synthetic source dataset and the provided target dataset are augmented to the training datasets to re-train the model. Since no monolingual corpus was provided in our case, we split the original dataset. To address any potential bias, we shuffled the dataset before splitting so that the created monolingual dataset is free from bias.

We also tried a variant of back translation called cyclic translation. The idea simply repeats the step of back-translation. After generating the synthetic source dataset from the provided target dataset, that dataset is used as input to the baseline source-to-target model to generate the synthetic target dataset. The synthetic source dataset and synthetic target dataset are augmented to the training datasets to train the model once again.

The shuffled back-translated model with a high drop-out rate and more number of training steps led to the highest BLEU score on the development dataset as reported in Section 5.

5 Experiment and Results

A lot of diverse models have been trained for our experiments as enumerated below which have been labeled as follows:

1. Baseline (Model 1)

2. Baseline with SQL keyword generalization (Model 2)

3. Baseline with SQL keyword generalization and true-cased input (Model 3)

Model	BLEU score on the dev set
Model 1	7.60
Model 2	9.72
Model 3	10.39
Model 4	11.05
Model 5	10.85
Model 6	10.46
Model 7	11.75
Model 8	9.50
Model 9	12.12

Table 2: Cross validation results with different models.

4. Back-translation with SQL keyword generalization and true-cased input (Model 4)

5. Cyclic-translation with SQL keyword generalization and true-cased input (Model 5)

6. Shuffled back-translation with SQL keyword generalization and true-cased input (Model 6)

7. Back-translation with SQL keyword generalization and true-cased input (higher dropout and more training steps) (Model 7)

8. Cyclic-translation with SQL keyword generalization and true-cased input (higher dropout and more training steps) (Model 8)

9. Shuffled back-translation with SQL keyword generalization and true-cased input and dropout rate = 0.5 (Model 9)

These models have been described in the previous sections. All the notable results are shown in Table 2.

We began our experiment by tuning the hyperparameters of the Seq2seq model in Tensorflow NMT. After repeated experimentation, we selected the parameters for our baseline training model (Model 1) as follows:

1. 4 layered bi-directional encoder

2. Source and target sequence length of 60

3. Adam optimizer

4. 0.001 as the initial learning rate

5. luong10 learning rate decay scheme as described in Tensorflow NMT

6. 12000 training steps

7. 0.4 drop-out rate

The other parameters are set to the default Tensorflow NMT values.

Then, we came up with the idea of SQL keyword generalization and implemented this idea. It turned out to be wonderful and improved the BLEU score significantly (from 7.60 to 9.72). Next, we focused on other possible pre-processing techniques that we could apply. We initially were considering four methods: tokenization, true-casing, linguistic factorization, and byte pair encoding. According to our testing, byte pair encoding, and the combination of these two methods degraded the BLEU score. Linguistic factorization led to high BLEU scores but the removal of the linguistic factors from the generated response again reduced the BLEU score. Tokenization also degrades the performance of the model. After carefully observing the given dataset, we found that it has already been tokenized, so further tokenization is unnecessary. In the end, SQL keyword generalization and true-casing are the two pre-processing techniques that we apply to the model.

Afterwards, we started to think about the steps in the training process that we could improve. We implemented back-translation, and it increased the BLEU score. However, we found this method is likely to introduce an overfitting issue. To be more specific, since we were not given any test data or any dataset analogous to a monolingual corpus, we split the given ground truth file for the development set into two files and used them (one as our "development" ground truth and the other as our "test" ground truth) for the external evaluation during the training. The model achieved a much higher BLEU score on our "development" ground truth than previously recorded but the BLEU score on our "test" ground truth decreased in comparison to that previously recorded.

Then, we came up with three ways to deal with this issue. The first one was the cyclic translation where no extra data (i.e. the monolingual data) is introduced in the training. This new way of training did help with the overfitting issue with a higher BLEU score on our created "test" dataset but failed to improve the BLEU score on the given development set. The second way was to shuffle the monolingual data used in the back-translation. It solved the overfitting issue but did not achieve a higher BLEU score on the development data either. The last way was to change the values for certain hyper-parameters. For instance, we increased the dropout rate from 0.4 to 0.5 to strengthen regularization. Accordingly, we also increased the number of training steps from 12000 to 20000. We applied the hyper-parameter changes to all three training methods, the original back-translation, cyclic translation, and shuffled back-translation. In the end, the shuffled back-translation model with the new hyper-parameter settings and the two pre-processing practices achieved the highest BLEU score on the development set.

6 Conclusion

Our submitted shuffled back-translation with a drop-out rate of 0.5 and 20000 training steps on Tensorflow NMT gives a BLEU score of 7.47 on the unknown testing dataset and a BLEU score of 12.12 on the development dataset. A further conclusion can be drawn once the Grammar and the Logical Consistency Rate (LCR) scores are released by the organizers. It can be observed that shuffled back-translation with a higher drop-out rate gave a high BLEU score on the development dataset compared to the baseline or the back-translated model with a lower drop-out rate. This suggests that the shuffling of the dataset before back-translation can potentially address the issue of any bias in the datasets. The improved results with increased drop-out suggest that regularization has been effective in this experimental setting. The idea of cyclic translation deserves further exploration. Generalization may be improved on the natural language responses by developing an improved variant of the linguistic factoring approach. The collection of additional training data can also be useful to increase the BLEU score on the unknown test dataset.

References

Saptarashmi Bandyopadhyay. 2019. Factored neural machine translation at loresmt 2019. In *Proceedings of the 2nd Workshop on Technologies for MT of Low Resource Languages*, pages 68–71.

Saptarashmi Bandyopadhyay. 2020. Factored neural machine translation on low resource languages in the covid-19 crisis.

Jim Gray, Surajit Chaudhuri, Adam Bosworth, Andrew Layman, Don Reichart, Murali Venkatrao, Frank Pellow, and Hamid Pirahesh. 1997. Data cube: A relational aggregation operator generalizing group-by, cross-tab, and sub-totals. *Data mining and knowledge discovery*, 1(1):29–53.

Vu Cong Duy Hoang, Philipp Koehn, Gholamreza Haffari, and Trevor Cohn. 2018. Iterative back-translation for neural machine translation. In *Proceedings of the 2nd Workshop on Neural Machine Translation and Generation*, pages 18–24.

Rico Sennrich, Barry Haddow, and Alexandra Birch. 2015. Improving neural machine translation models with monolingual data. *arXiv preprint arXiv:1511.06709*.

Richard Shin. 2019. Encoding database schemas with relation-aware self-attention for text-to-sql parsers. *arXiv preprint arXiv:1906.11790*.

Tao Yu, Rui Zhang, He Yang Er, Suyi Li, Eric Xue, Bo Pang, Xi Victoria Lin, Yi Chern Tan, Tianze Shi, Zihan Li, et al. 2019. Cosql: A conversational text-to-sql challenge towards cross-domain natural language interfaces to databases. *arXiv preprint arXiv:1909.05378*.

Xiaoshi Zhong, Aixin Sun, and Erik Cambria. 2017. Time expression analysis and recognition using syntactic token types and general heuristic rules. In *Proceedings of the 55th Annual Meeting of the Association for Computational Linguistics (Volume 1: Long Papers)*, pages 420–429, Vancouver, Canada. Association for Computational Linguistics.

Association for Computational Linguistics
209 N. Eighth Street
Stroudsburg, Pennsylvania 18360

ISBN 978-1-7138-1986-8

CURRAN ASSOCIATES INC.
proceedings.com